LUTHERAN
VOICES

Called by God to Serve
Reflections for Church Leaders

Paul E. Walters and Robert F. Holley

Augsburg Fortress

Minneapolis

CALLED BY GOD TO SERVE
Reflections for Church Leaders

Scripture quotations unless otherwise noted are from the New Revised Standard Version Bible, copyright © 1989 Division of Christian Education of the National Council of Churches of Christ in the United States of America. Used by permission.

Direct quotations from Martin Luther's Small Catechism are from *A Contemporary Translation of Luther's Small Catechism*, Pocket Edition. Introduction and translation by Timothy J. Wingert. Copyright © 1996 Augsburg Fortress. Used by Permission.

Editor: Thomas S. Hanson

Cover photo: © Royalty-Free/CORBIS

Library of Congress Cataloging-in-Publication Data
Walters, Paul E.
  Called by God to serve : reflections for church leaders / Paul E. Walters and Bob Holley.
    p. cm. -- (Lutheran voices)
  ISBN 0-8066-5172-5 (alk. paper)
  1. Christian leadership. I. Holley, Bob. II. Title. III. Series.
  BV652.1.W35 2004
  253--dc22
                              2004014830

The paper used in this publication meets the minimum requirements of American National Standard for Information Sciences—Permanence of Paper for Printed Library Materials, ANSI Z329.48-1984.

Manufactured in the U.S.A.   ISBN 0-8066-5172-5
08   07   06   05   2   3   4   5   6   7   8   9   10

Contents

Preface

You are a church council member. You have been called by God to serve faithfully and diligently in Christ's holy church. All the baptized belong to the "priesthood of all believers," as Lutherans speak of the church. This statement means all people have equal access to God. Belonging to the priesthood of all believers also means all the baptized are priests and servants of God; you have been called by God to serve the church as a council member.

Sometimes the demands of this calling as a council member are unclear. Often, there is not a job description, or a clear list of responsibilities for a council member, or even a training session. This ambiguity leads to confusion and frequently causes leaders to spend too much time trying to figure out what they are asked to do rather than being the leaders they are called to be.

Maybe you served on the community swimming pool board or the PTA and said to yourself, "I know how to be a board member." Serving on church council is different from other councils, however, because of who members serve and who calls them to serve.

These reflections will challenge you with God's call. It is often tempting to spend most council meetings managing the finances of the congregation. But what of the congregation's mission? You will be reminded that the purpose of the church is not to perpetuate itself, but to serve God's holy purpose in this broken and hurting world.

These reflections explore what it means to be a leader in the church. The Holy Scriptures lie at the heart of each reflection. Some reflections are essays with discussion questions at the conclusion. Other reflections begin with a true-to-life story from the parish, then follow with discussion questions, and conclude with a scripture text and a response.

This resource can be used as devotions to begin council meetings each month for three years, with a break during the summer months. In this way you might start with chapter 1 and continue for three years to chapter 30. You might prefer to pick and choose topics depending on the situation in your congregation. Several chapters could be used together to form the basis for a leadership retreat.

However you choose to make use of the book, remember this: the most important information is not found in the pages of the book. The most important and significant learning will come from you and your congregation. As you respond to the situations presented and wrestle with the discussion questions, you will learn and grow and be changed. As you discuss the challenges that have faced other congregations, it is the authors' prayer that you will be better equipped to respond in your own setting when challenges arise.

These reflections express ideas born from systems theory. This way of thinking understands that we live in a world defined by relationships and interconnections, not simply by cause and effect. It is not just what is said, but also how it is responded to that makes the difference. Cause-and-effect thinking can be illustrated by kicking a large rock. When you kick a large rock the rock does not respond. If you kick a dog, however, the dog will respond. Whether the dog runs away or tries to bite you determines your next move. This is a system.

Any group of people living and working together forms a system. You experience this at work, in your family, and in your congregation. Everything anyone does has an impact on the rest of the system. Change in one part will be felt in other parts of the system. The fire in Mary's kitchen is a prime example (chapter 26). Mary was not hurt and, while her kitchen needed to be replaced, the house was unharmed. Yet this relatively small fire caused great problems in her congregation. Why? It seemed Mary always baked all the bread for Holy Communion. Without Mary's kitchen someone else had to bake the bread. The recipe they used was different. Other hands kneaded the dough. All these necessary changes caused great anxiety. This is a system.

Most likely, you have many similar examples of interconnectedness in the life of your congregation. In these reflections we will consider relationships between people and programs within congregations. In considering these interactions, you will discover how the system of your congregation functions. These insights will provide you with additional tools to lead your congregation.

As council members you are the leaders of your congregation. Your sisters and brothers in Christ have prayerfully asked you to lead your congregation. As leaders you are in the position to model healthy relationships and faithful living. As leaders you have the opportunity to challenge your congregation so it might grow in faithfulness.

May God bless you and your conversation and study that you may prove faithful and diligent servants in Christ's holy church.

Paul Walters and Bob Holley
The Season of Pentecost 2004

Acknowledgments

We give thanks to God for the many people who have supported us in this endeavor.

For those who have traveled the journey with us: Janet, Michelle, and Allison; Brandy, Nicholas, and Nathan, our families. They wondered about and were not certain why we met each Wednesday for months on end.

For the Collegium, Chris Carr, Bob Clarke, Al Fogelman, Dianna Horton, Bob Humphrey, Randy Lohr, Shari Shull, and Jan Tobias. One free breakfast hardly compensates for your critique, suggestions, teasing, and editing, but it will have to do.

We give thanks to God for Scott Tunseth, who very early in the project believed this book had the potential to serve the church.

We give thanks for the numerous believers on the journey who generously gave of themselves that this book might be written, especially Duane Osheim.

We trust what we have done is faithful to the Gospel of Jesus Christ and will strengthen congregational leaders as they serve with their lives.

Year One

The Church as a Journey

In the next ten chapters, you will go on a great journey. You will travel from the hot desert sands of Mount Sinai, to the shores of Galilee, through the belly of the great fish, to the first days of the church after the day of Pentecost, to the garden of the resurrection of our Lord, and back to the early church. Each month you will be challenged to expand your vision for the church, for your congregation, and for the journey you are on together.

As leaders of the church, you will be called on to respond to complaints and criticisms. God's promised future gives us hope when the anger and frustrations of the moment tear us down. Looking toward God's future, we can understand complaints as an opportunity for conversation and growth.

We are called to care for one another in our journey, but that is not where it ends. We are also a sent people. We are sent into the cities, towns, and villages of the whole world. There is no one outside our concern. Our Lord commands us to "go and make disciples of all nations" (Matthew 28:19). Yet this is not always an easy or pleasant task.

Serving as a leader of a group of people, even "good church folk," is not an easy calling. Some days it takes all your strength. Through these reflections it is the author's prayer that you will grow in your understanding of God's call in your life and your mutual journey.

The need for long-term vision and goals—planning for the journey—should also be clear. These goals and plans will give you something vital and significant to discuss each month. You can point others in the direction of faithfulness to God's call. United as the people of God, sharing a vision of hope, trusting in God for comfort and strength, you will be faithfully serving.

1

The Gods We Worship

Read Exodus 32:1-6

When people bring their problems to the council meeting we become anxious. We feel the pressures of the problems and we want them to go away and will do anything to make that happen. If we forget, like Aaron and the Israelites, whose we are, we will worship anyone or anything. We will create our own calf of gold. There are all sorts of people and things to choose from to become our idol, including the pastor, the building, the organ, what is successful and popular in other churches, or the whims of members. If we do not have clear goals, we give in to the pressures of the moment. We often worry about what is urgent, not what is important.

Exodus 32 is a story of faithlessness. No sooner did Moses go up the mountain than the people of Israel got nervous and anxious. Aaron's response was to provide them something comfortable and common. Aaron gave the Israelites a god to worship that was anything but the true God.

The calling for council members is to faithfulness. It begins with the word of God, "I am the Lord your God. You shall have no other gods." The calf made of gold is a classic illustration of this. Moses did not relieve the anxiety of the people, so in their impatience they begged Aaron to take care of them. He was more than willing to help. He provided a quick and easy solution. The problem with his solution was that it was unfaithful.

Moses, on the other hand, faithfully interceded with God for the people. As the story continues, Moses begs God not to seek revenge on the people of Israel for their unfaithfulness. He pleads and God relents. Forgiveness and grace are God's way.

In Aaron and Moses we have two people who could well be

members of our council. Aaron is the person who is quick to solve the problems. Moses is the council member who tries to thoughtfully and prayerfully reflect on what God desires of us before choosing a path to walk. Idols are still being made when we beg "Aaron" to take away our discomfort and our anxiety with a quick solution.

Success is one of the idols that replace a relationship with God. Many councils have made rash and quick decisions to imitate another church or organization. "If only we focus on the youth, our problems will be solved. That is what they do at Valley Church." It sounds so easy, so clear, and so within reach. We gather the gold rings and make the calf.

Another idol is the church as a club. When impatience and anxiety rises we often hear, "We need to take care of ourselves." Mission is dropped, benevolence and outreach are the least of our worries. We need to survive, and all activity focuses inward, attempting to resuscitate the dying body. Without saying it, we think of the country club or another organization and how well they do when they focus on their members. We gather the gold rings and make the calf.

Some idols come well disguised. When we worship them we get stuck. How many councils have spent ten or fifteen minutes discussing where to get the best price on toilet paper and which brand is best? If our focus is on keeping the peace at all costs, the congregation will rarely experience positive change. How often do you run out of time to deal with significant issues?

How do we act faithfully?

God calls us to faithfulness, not to success by the world's standards. Seeking God's will requires patience. Spend time each month at your council meeting discovering what God is calling your congregation to become. This is one of the most important functions of a council. Develop clear goals and plans for the future. This becomes your mission and ministry. Have vision.

Listen first to God and the gift of the gospel. In the cross of Jesus Christ your salvation has been guaranteed. It is a gift of grace. You need not worry about doing things to qualify. You can trust God for that gift. Listen as well to the people of God. As they ask things of you, carefully consider their requests. Is what they ask something that will fit your congregation's goals and plans?

As your council develops plans and goals, it is essential to communicate these to the congregation. Clear communication allows the members to know your council is listening and responding.

To be called by God to serve as a member of council means living in the grace that calls us to trust God. When anxiety and impatience come to us from members of the congregation, we do not react. Rather, we prayerfully and thoughtfully consider requests to see if they are part of our mission and ministry.

Questions

1. What idols or "calves of gold" tempt you as leaders?

2. What do you deliberately do to focus on the mission of the congregation?

3. How does your council react when anxiety rises in your congregation?

2

Joyful Generosity

Read Matthew 6:1-6, 16-21

Like it or not, church councils deal with money. Each month you
get the treasurer's report. Are you ahead or behind this month?
Every autumn comes the budget, which gets bigger every year. How
will you ever raise the money for the budget?

Jesus calls us to faithful obedience. Giving alms, prayer, and fasting all assume we have a trusting relationship with God. We trust
that in Jesus Christ God has come to us and made us children of
God. By God's initiative and grace we live in a loving relationship
with God. There is no other way.

Our relationship with money and the power it has over our lives
is crucial to our relationship with God. Money, and all it can get for
us, can easily become our god. To guard against this, we talk about
"receiving an offering" rather than "taking the collection." On behalf
of God, the church receives gifts given in faith. This reminds us that
only God is God.

In Matthew's Gospel, "alms" refers to money (v. 2), money given
for the care of the poor. From Scripture, we know proportional giving of money is the calling of the faithful steward. Some people refer
to this giving as a *tithe*. A tithe is a gift of 10 percent of one's
income. But, it is not critical your gift be exactly 10 percent.
Proportional giving means determining beforehand what your percentage will be, then faithfully giving it. Hopefully we challenge
ourselves over the years and the percentage will increase.

Faithful stewardship will greatly relieve the stress of council
members. The budget will take care of itself. Giving just to pay the
bills will suck the vitality and energy of a congregation dry. Faithful

stewardship—taught, witnessed to, and practiced—will strengthen the spiritual health of the congregation.

Generosity of possessions leads us to generosity of time. When the council discusses the budget for the coming year, everyone has some insight to offer. We understand how money works in our families. We spend what we must and then we try and put a little aside, build up some reserves, and prepare for the future. If we apply these same standards to the finances of the church, we may not be faithful stewards. In the church our priority is not accumulating but giving.

Jesus calls us to faithfulness in all aspects of life. One part of that is financial, but there are other important aspects of life. Prayer is a time-consuming activity. Each day we lay aside time for listening and speaking to God. We use this time to deepen and strengthen our relationship with God. Our time might be spent in the service of others. Our serving becomes prayer. This is contrary to the way of the world, and is a holy calling. Generosity of possessions and time leads to generosity toward self for the sake of others. Fasting reminds us to ask: Are we meeting our wants to the detriment of faithful serving? Fasting takes us to a time of reflection, helping us order our priorities so our needs are met and others are served. Faithful priorities are part of being a steward.

How do we serve faithfully?

As stewards of the congregation, council members are called by God to follow the instructions of our Lord Jesus regarding prayer, fasting, and alms-giving.

The people of God gather in prayer, continually seeking God's guidance, having the patience to wait for an answer in God's own good time. Fast from the need to find a quick answer. Fast from the need to judge the church's finances according to the world's standards. Spend money wisely, but faithfully; trusting that God will continue to care for the congregation long after your time of service has ended.

The people of God give their resources generously. They seek out ways to share what they have. You might invite groups from the community to use your facility. They might not even think to ask, so you offer.

The people of God consider ways that generous giving is spiritually healthy. How are people blessed through generosity? How can the council help others receive these blessings? What keeps people from being generous? How can the council remove the barriers to generosity in the congregation?

For the people of God, stewardship is the care of creation and the care of money. Stewardship is care of our bodies as well as the annual budget. The council is called to encourage stewardship in all aspects of life.

Consider ways as a congregation that you can reflect the breadth of stewardship.

To be called by God to serve as a council member means you have a responsibility to the entire congregation, living as a model of faithfulness and providing others with opportunities for generosity. It means you are called to encourage others in faithfulness through prayer, fasting, and alms-giving. It means living in grace and trusting fully in the faithfulness of the God who calls us by name.

Questions

1. Are you comfortable discussing money in council meetings? Why or why not?

2. What barriers keep people from being generous?

3. How can the council remove these barriers to generosity in the congregation?

3

Sin in the Church

Read Matthew 18:15-22

As leaders of the congregation, council members have a responsibility to lead and to confront their individual and corporate shortcomings. The council also must work to prevent the back-biting that can eat away at a community. In the passage from Matthew, Jesus provides clear instructions on how we should speak to and about one another. Clear communication is one of the basic responsibilities of a council member. Part of this is listening well to others. Part of this is not talking about others, but talking to them.

Jesus outlines a three-step approach to conflict: first, speak directly, one to one; second, bring two or three others along for the second conversation; and third, tell the entire church. As you follow these three steps remember this process is all about forgiveness, not about proving who is right and who is wrong.

Direct communication is not easy. Our Lord is clear in his response to our sin. If another sins against you, go to her or him directly. Go to listen, not to argue. Go intending to heal a damaged relationship. If your goal is only to get your way, you have lost before you begin.

If you are not listened to initially, bring another person or two with you. With prayer and patience maybe three or four people can see hope where two did not. Go humbly. Go with prayer. Go with mercy and compassion. Go to regain a friend.

Our Lord speaks clearly to us. The path to healing is the light of openness, not the darkness of secrets. God's mercy and compassion, revealed through the gift of Jesus, light the path of healing.

Upon hearing the call to forgive, Peter asks Jesus how many times one is expected to forgive another. Peter thinks seven times is more than enough. Jesus tells Peter, "Not seven times, but, I tell you, seventy-seven times" (v. 22). In other words, forgive and forgive again. Following the instruction of our Lord Jesus, we love another back into relationship.

Clear communication requires speaking directly to one another. Gossip means talking about others, not to them. Gossip is sin. Gossip is destructive to others. When others approach you with gossip, politely suggest that they need to talk directly to the person. Encourage conversation that builds up relationships.

Is it gossip? Try this test. If you would not feel comfortable asking a person a question directly, maybe it is not a question you should be asking someone else about them. Most likely this is gossip.

Words have great power. You can use words to build up the people of God. It is a holy calling as council members to use words to build up others. Speak well of others, encourage them, compliment them, give them confidence through your words.

People will sin against you. Maybe even before you get the chance to sin against them. Relationships require forgiveness. Our Lord knows we do not always treat one another well. We are not always kind. We are not always faithful.

We can also sin by keeping silent. Even in the church we keep secrets from one another. Even in the church we bear grudges. We keep silent during council meetings, refusing to voice our opinion. Sometimes the "real meeting" is in the parking lot after the first meeting ends. We are not always direct and honest with one another. All of this is destructive in the life of a congregation.

Secrets prevent healing. Secrets control us when important discussions take place in the parking lot after the council meeting or on the phone the next day. Gossip controls us when we talk *about* one another and not *to* one another.

How do we live faithfully?

Speak directly to others, not about others. This is not always easy to do. Be careful with your words. Pay attention to what is happening in a conversation. Is it gossip or communication? You will need to decide and act accordingly.

Forgive others. Jesus calls us to forgive when we have been offended. This means an appropriate apology, repentance, and penance. Do not forget this when you have been the one who offended another.

Seek ways to encourage others and build them up with your words. By building up others you build up the church, and the ministry and mission of your congregation will grow.

Health will grow in a congregation when there is openness and clarity. The faithful council member will be direct and open with others. The faithful council member will find the courage from God to forgive.

To be called by God to serve as a member of council means living in the grace that calls us to trust God. In all conversation and communication, strive to speak to people, not about them. As you continue to forgive others you build up the people of God.

Questions

1. How can council meetings be places for open and honest discussion?

2. How have you seen secrets damage relationships? Has this happened in your congregation?

3. How can the council encourage honest open communication throughout the congregation?

4

The Burden of Leadership

Read Isaiah 9:2, 4-5

²The people who walked in darkness have seen a great light; those who lived in a land of deep darkness—on them light has shined.

⁴For the yoke of their burden, and the bar across their shoulders, the rod of their oppressor, you have broken as on the day of Midian. ⁵For all the boots of the tramping warriors and all the garments rolled in blood shall be burned as fuel for the fire.

You probably were not told this before you were elected: as a council member you are a person who is called to hear complaints. You hear concerns and frustrations. Those who are not comfortable going directly to others with their difficulties and concerns may well bring them to you. They may expect you to solve their problems. It might feel like an army is encamped against you.

In these times, being a council member can become a burden. Faithful living is not an easy calling. Responding graciously to complaints is a difficult skill to master. If the initiative were all our responsibility it would be impossible to live faithfully.

We can thank God that we do not have to live faithfully by our own initiative. We do not serve because we want to. We serve because the Holy Spirit calls us to serve. We live faithfully, strengthened by God's grace.

In Isaiah 9, the prophet promises those who have suffered great trouble that they will be delivered. The light will shine on their great darkness. We know that even the light of a single candle can pierce the darkness. When we baptize, the new Christian is often given a candle that represents that this newly baptized person is now part of the church, and therefore, part of the witnessing community. We are all called in Baptism to proclaim the saving grace of God through our words and actions.

Isaiah tells us that we can celebrate because God turns our darkness to light. What burdens and oppresses us, what imprisons us, will be broken by God (v. 4). We will be set free. That is good and gracious news. It is God's doing.

The boots and uniforms of armies will be burned (v. 5). God will give perpetual peace. There will be no war anymore. So you can burn the boots and uniforms. It is God's doing.

Finally, we rejoice because God is sending us a king who will bring the kingdom of God to us. God's will is made flesh in the weakest of human creatures—a little baby—bringing peace, justice, and righteousness. We know this baby-king as our Lord Jesus, thus we often hear this text each Advent season.

Advent is a season of preparation. During early winter days, we prepare our hearts for the joyful celebration of Christ's birth. These words from Isaiah tell of our past and our future. Isaiah reminds us of those days in life when we live under a crushing load of work and responsibilities. These are dark days, days when we hear nothing but complaints and demands. Isaiah reminds us of these days and weeks in life where sin reigns supreme in our lives.

In these days, God makes faithful service possible. Even in difficult and frustrating times, we have faith in God's promised future. We trust our burden will be lifted, peace will reign, and the Christ child will bring God's kingdom. Even as we live in darkness we know the light of Christ pierces the gloom. We look with hope to the future, knowing that because God has promised peace and joy it is as good as here.

How do we live faithfully?

We live faithfully by paying attention to the powerful theme of preparation as emphasized in the season of Advent. Advent leads us to prepare for the future, trusting in God's continuing presence and care. Plan boldly for the future. Look with confidence to the coming months and years. Look to God to sustain your congregation.

Isaiah's words are filled with optimism and hope. As Advent people, consider your own congregation. Where is there darkness? Where does the light of Christ need to shine? These are places for preparation. These are places to declare the gospel.

Where is your congregation strong and vital? How is your congregation shining the light of Christ into the world? These are strengths to be celebrated. These are joys to be shared. Consider how your congregation can celebrate its strengths and successes.

Look with confidence to God and consider these questions: What is God preparing this congregation for? Who is God calling you to become?

To be called by God to serve as a council member means to trust in God as you plan for the future: Shine light into darkness. Celebrate God's presence among you. Follow where God leads you. Look with faith and confidence to God who sustains us throughout our lives and guarantees us a future in the kingdom.

Questions

1. How have you responded to complaints as a council member?

2. What are the strengths of your congregation?

3. How else might God use us to combine these strengths in service in the world?

5
The Heart of Faith

Read Matthew 28:16-20

What is at the heart of our faith? Is it reaching out to others in the name of Jesus Christ? Does this make you a disciple? We witness and educate in hopes of being instruments as God makes disciples. In these concluding words of Matthew's Gospel, Jesus reminds the disciples of his authority, and then he sends them out into the world with specific instructions and a word of promise.

Churches are wonderful places. They offer an opportunity to hear God's word and receive the sacraments. In congregations we make friends, maybe some of our closest friends. We invest time, money, and energy in our congregations. We serve with our lives. We are cared for when illness or tragedy strikes. We care for others in their distress. Yet, amid all the good and faithful deeds of any congregation, there also lies a danger.

If our reason for gathering as a church is simply to get our needs met, we are in trouble. This reason can be hard to detect. People may be serving faithfully in the life of the congregation and there may be countless volunteer hours already accumulated. But what are they doing? Does the energy and hard work focus on the congregation and the members alone? Is maintaining what you have a higher priority than serving outside the congregation?

Our Lord reminds us that when we serve ourselves first, we have forgotten who called us together. When we care for ourselves only, we have forgotten who gave us the authority to gather at all.

We are not called to worship for our sake alone; we worship for the benefit of the world. In the prayers of the faithful, *Lutheran Book of Worship* reminds us, "Prayers are included for the whole Church, the nations, those in need, the parish [and] special concerns" (*LBW*, p. 106). Our prayers look outward long before they look inward.

In the same way, our congregation is called to follow the command of our Lord Jesus: "*Go* therefore and *make disciples* of all nations, *baptizing them* in the name of the Father and of the Son and of the Holy Spirit" (Matthew 28:19; *italics added*). These active commands from our Lord are not always followed. We call these words of Jesus the "great commission." Plainly, Jesus says that disciples are instruments of God's choosing in the process of making others disciples.

Witnessing is a difficult challenge, but it is at the center of what our congregation is to be about as the people of God. Christ calls us into mission, and our purpose is to introduce others to Christ so that they might live in a faithful relationship with him.

The chrismon (Christmas tree ornaments) cross for Epiphany is the Jerusalem cross. It is a cross that has equal arms extending from the center and a small crossbar on the end of each of the arms. Thus, when you look at the Jerusalem cross, you see a cross made up of four smaller crosses, the base of each coming together at the center of the larger cross.

Why four small crosses? Look at Matthew 28. Jesus tells his disciples to go from Jerusalem to the world and witness to the gospel. In Jesus' time and ours, we often think of the world as having four corners, North, South, East, and West. The four-corners cross reminds us we are called to go to everyone, everywhere.

How do we live faithfully?

Begin to live faithfully by hearing God's word and receiving the sacraments. This will propel us out into the world. God's word will push us out of our comfort zone and challenge us in amazing ways.

As a council, ask yourselves what it is that leads and guides the actions of your members. Ask yourselves if witnessing is the central purpose for your church. Is proclamation of the gospel always the priority?

Learning is important. What classes or workshops have you provided to members that will help them to witness? Part of being instruments that make disciples is to teach them. Proclaiming Jesus Christ as Lord needs to be the top priority. How do we help disciples do that?

Example is important as well. Do you invite others to worship with you? Do you invite others to Bible study and other learning opportunities? The general membership of the congregation will only do what the leaders are willing to do. What kind of an example are you?

To be called by God to serve as a council member is to have a responsibility to provide your congregation with opportunities to follow Jesus' command. Pray for wisdom. Look at the needs around you and consider the pain of the world. God has provided you with talents and abilities to witness where you are.

Questions

1. How is your congregation faithfully responding to the great commission?

2. At what points does your congregation turn inward and care only for itself?

3. How can the council keep proclamation of the gospel a priority for the congregation?

6

Apathy in the Church

Read Jonah 3:1-10; 4:1

The Holy Spirit sometimes calls us to unpleasant and embarrassing tasks. Jonah is called by the Holy Spirit to such a task. Jonah's call is one of the great stories of the Bible. Jonah's life reminds us God's grace is sufficient.

God calls Jonah to preach in Nineveh, the capital city of the enemy. Jonah responds by getting on a boat heading in the opposite direction. God sends a terrible storm that ends when the crew follows Jonah's suggestion and tosses him into the sea. Once in the water, God sends a huge fish to swallow Jonah. After three days in the belly of the fish, Jonah pleads to God in prayer for release. Graciously, the fish vomits Jonah up on dry land.

Now, God calls Jonah a second time. This time Jonah obeys God. He preaches to the people of Nineveh and the king repents. All the people repent. Even the animals repent. God's response is gracious and forgiving.

You would think Jonah would be delighted. Instead, he is furious with God. Recall, Jonah complained from the beginning that he did not want to serve. Jonah's pride made him angry when God spoke through him and the people repented.

Jonah's tale is retold because, like Jonah, there are times when we are reluctant to answer God's call. There are days when it seems as though our congregations are filled with Jonahs. There are days when we discover Jonah in our hearts. People may hear the call of God, but there is just so much to be done. Jobs, children, homes, cars, and hobbies are all competing for time and energy. When the church is just one more item on the list, it will often be overlooked.

How many phone calls does it take to find three new church

council members for the coming year? How many people decline God's call to serve as council president or as a Sunday school teacher? How about that time you were asked to be chair of the stewardship committee, teach Sunday school, or serve as an assisting minister? Did you beg off because you were too busy? Did you refuse because it seemed to be something you wouldn't want to do? Did you try, like Jonah, to escape God's call to serve in this way? Do we live in the shadow of Jonah?

Jonah is not particularly faithful. Jonah does not even seem to care about being faithful. Jonah does not hate God; he just does not want to be bothered. How often does apathy seem to win the day in your congregation?

This issue goes far beyond the call to serve on committees or in the leadership of a congregation. How do we respond to the call to discipleship? Are we learning continuously? Are we witnessing again and again or are we as reluctant as Jonah?

We consider Jonah because, while Jonah is reluctant, God is persistent. While Jonah is stubborn, God is steadfast. God refuses to let Jonah go, no matter how many times Jonah says, "No, not me." This is how God works. God is relentless. God is totally committed to us, even when we are mired in the muck of apathy.

Reluctance is frustrating for those who have been captured by the great vision of the gospel. You might be tempted to become cynical. If our efforts alone would cure this malaise, the repeated failure would be devastating.

God looks patiently for the right time. God will take extreme measures to accomplish the divine will. Jonah had to live in the belly of a fish for three days and be vomited onto the shore before he would submit to God's will. We pray most people are less reluctant than Jonah.

How do we live faithfully?

As a council member be consistent in your use of the means of grace. By regular worship you are fed by the Word of God and the Lord's Supper. Daily search the Scriptures in study and reflection. Prayer will draw you closer to God through Christ. This will nurture and sustain your relationship with God.

Serving as a council member calls for faith and patience. Have faith that God will continue to sustain your congregation. Have faith that God will transform reluctance to passion. Be patient waiting for God's right time.

Listen for the times God calls you to Nineveh, to those places you don't want to go. It may be the chair of a committee; it may be sharing your faith with a stranger. Whatever it is, the call is yours to respond to as a disciple in faith, trusting God will give you all you need to complete the task.

To be called by God to serve as a church council member means to look to God for patience and confidence. Share the great vision of the gospel, trusting in the Holy Spirit to stir up the hearts of God's people.

Questions

1. To what difficult task has God called you or your congregation?

2. How has your congregation avoided a task to which God is calling you?

3. What has happened when you have completed the unpleasant task?

7

The Gift of God's Word

Read Acts 2:38-42

> [38]Peter said to them, "Repent, and be baptized every one of you in the name of Jesus Christ so that your sins may be forgiven; and you will receive the gift of the Holy Spirit. [39]For the promise is for you, for your children, and for all who are far away, everyone whom the Lord our God calls to him." [40]And he testified with many other arguments and exhorted them, saying, "Save yourselves from this corrupt generation." [41]So those who welcomed his message were baptized, and that day about three thousand persons were added. [42]They devoted themselves to the apostles' teaching and fellowship, to the breaking of bread and the prayers.

What do you think the early church was like? How was it different from your church? The text from Acts 2 contains a sermon by Peter as the church begins. Acts provides us with a glimpse of the church as it could be.

In verse 42, we read that the first Christians "devoted themselves to the apostles' teaching and fellowship, to the breaking of the bread and the prayers." This is an outline of a Christian church like yours, the one your council oversees.

We gather to hear God's word through the reading of Scripture and preaching. We celebrate Holy Communion and we pray. This is Christian worship, the public celebration of the faith of the church.

When Martin Luther explained the third commandment in his Small Catechism, he did not become legalistic about Sunday worship. Luther wrote that the commandment, "Remember the sabbath day, and keep it holy" means, "We are to fear and love God, so that we do not despise God's Word or preaching, but instead keep that Word holy and gladly hear and learn it." Notice how he did not speak of just Sunday morning, the Christian sabbath. Luther felt that keeping the sabbath was to turn daily to the gift of God's word.

God's word includes Holy Baptism. In Baptism all believers have received forgiveness of sins and a place at the kingdom table. The word of God is present "with, in, and among" the water, so forgiveness is a gracious gift of God. We baptize in the name of the triune God, knowing the promise of forgiveness and life in the kingdom.

God's word also comes in the Lord's Supper, the meal of forgiveness. Christ is present in the meal, forgiving us and strengthening us for service to all people. The Word is Christ, and we experience the Word under the forms of bread and wine, the body and blood of Christ, gifts of grace.

Proclamation is also God's word, and not only in sermons. Daily use of God's word and regular Sunday worship combine to feed us the word of forgiveness that falls upon our ears, once again a gift. If we are not present to God's word, it cannot speak to us.

Thus, worship forms and grounds us. Worship teaches us whose we are and what we believe. Many of the good works of a congregation, from feeding the hungry to caring for children, are mirrored by nonreligious organizations. What makes us different as Christians is not only what we do, but in whose name we act.

Throughout our lives our faith is renewed and strengthened through worship. The gathered community hearing the word of God, receiving the sacraments, praying for all those in need, and caring for one another is the church. The church has no physical location. The church is the gathered body of Christ around word and sacraments.

How do we live faithfully?

As a council, do as Luther suggests: be attentive to God's word and the preaching of it. Do not despise it. Gladly hear and learn it.

If worship provides our grounding, begin your council meetings with worship and not only prayer. "Responsive Prayer II" in *Lutheran Book of Worship* (p. 164) is an excellent option. Read Scripture, sing a simple hymn, share your faith, pray together.

As a council, it is your responsibility along with your pastor to see that the word of God is preached, and that the sacraments are regularly offered to the people of God. These are the means of grace, the forms through which God brings the word to us.

There are other opportunities for learning the word: confirmation class, Bible studies, meetings, Sunday school, and so forth. Support and encourage these moments. They are times for the word to be heard.

To be called by God to serve as a council member means to be attentive to the word of God. Daily, draw close to the word and let it speak to you. Be at worship, gathering, hearing God's word, sharing in the meal, and praying. Encourage others to do the same.

Questions

1. How does God's word speak to you each day?

2. What is an example of a decision you made differently because you are a church council and not a secular organization?

3. How do you ensure that your faith informs your decisions?

8

Christ Is Risen!
He Is Risen Indeed!

Read John 20:11-18

You know the Easter story well. You have heard it many times. It is so familiar that sometimes you lose the impact of what great news the resurrection brings. Christ is risen. You are promised new life, a place at the table with Jesus in the coming kingdom. This is astounding news. It is the best announcement you will ever hear. "I have seen the Lord!" are words echoing in our lives every day, reminding us God comes to us and with unconditional love provides the victory of life over death.

This is something to celebrate. This is why Easter is a week of Sundays in the church calendar (seven weeks). Christ is risen and life is never the same. Alleluia!

We celebrate this joy, but it is too great to contain. We also tell others. For council members, Easter is a reminder of why the church exists. As Jesus sent Mary to go and tell the others, he also sends us to go and tell the good news of his resurrection. Go and tell the promise of life we now have, even in death. Alleluia!

Unfortunately, we easily forget our calling. We move from becoming a gathered people who go out to proclaim the good news to an institution more concerned about self-preservation, a club. We turn in upon ourselves and find it is easier to become a club than it is to answer the call to tell others. Every congregation faces this struggle. Responsible council members will remind themselves and others we are the church, not a club.

As council members you are called to care for the spiritual needs of your congregation. As faithful leaders, you and your pastors are called to be vigilant so that the means of grace are properly and regularly made available to the entire congregation—this includes God's word as it is preached, taught, and sung, and the sacraments of Holy Baptism and the Lord's Supper.

Consider what accommodations might be made for those with difficulty hearing the preached word. Consider how frequently Holy Communion is offered. Look for ways to remind people of the daily nature of Baptism. Consider how lay members might help distribute Communion to homebound members more frequently than the pastor is able to do alone.

You are called by God to care for the entire community and place the good of all ahead of your own opinions and feelings. This is not always easy. No calling from God is ever easy.

As a council member you are called by God to seek out ways your congregation can share the love and grace of God with those who are in desperate need. Those who are poor and those who are hungry are your concern. Those who are abused and neglected, all those suffering in your midst, are your concern. You are called to discover ways to lead your congregation to faithfully care for those in need.

Even as you do all these things in response to the gracious God who loves and cares for you, there remains one thing more: you are called to forgive as you have been forgiven. As a leader in the church, you are called to model forgiveness in your congregation. This means forgiving your friend when you have been wronged. This means forgiving those people with whom you do not get along—those within and outside the church.

How do we live faithfully?

Trust the gift of life you have in Jesus. Live the gospel freedom that through the death and resurrection of Jesus God has saved you. You do not have to qualify. You do not have to make some kind of decision or say the right thing. God has done what is needed for this life and one more.

Trust that God truly forgives you. The death and resurrection of our Lord brings you the forgiveness of all your sins. It gives you a new status: child of God, forgiven by and reconciled to God. Love as you have been loved. Forgive as you have been forgiven. Live with compassion and mercy.

Trust that God is calling you and all the church to tell others this wonderful news. Focus on that truth. Work so everyone learns to use their own voice for sharing the good news. See that your church offers opportunities for members to enrich their lives in the gospel so they may enrich others. Responsibly provide for the spiritual care of your congregation.

To be called by God to serve as a council member means to trust God to deliver on the Easter promise. Trust God that all has been accomplished to provide your future at the kingdom table, now and forever. Trust God that the Holy Spirit will nourish you and provide what you need to tell others. You are on the path to fulfilling your calling as a council member.

Questions

1. How do you determine whether the spiritual needs of the congregation are being met?

2. What spiritual needs of the congregation go unmet? How might you care for these needs?

3. How has the Easter story changed your life?

9

Variety in the Body of Christ

Read 1 Corinthians 12:4-13, 27

[4]Now there are varieties of gifts, but the same Spirit; [5]and there are varieties of services, but the same Lord; [6]and there are varieties of activities, but it is the same God who activates all of them in everyone. [7]To each is given the manifestation of the Spirit for the common good. [8]To one is given through the Spirit the utterance of wisdom, and to another the utterance of knowledge according to the same Spirit, [9]to another faith by the same Spirit, to another gifts of healing by the one Spirit, [10]to another the working of miracles, to another prophecy, to another the discernment of spirits, to another various kinds of tongues, to another the interpretation of tongues. [11]All these are activated by one and the same Spirit, who allots to each one individually just as the Spirit chooses.

[12]For just as the body is one and has many members, and all the members of the body, though many, are one body, so it is with Christ. [13]For in the one Spirit we were all baptized into one body—Jews or Greeks, slaves or free—and we were all made to drink of one Spirit.

[27]Now you are the body of Christ and individually members of it.

How do you grapple with differences? Do you look for and encourage variety in your congregation? The apostle Paul, writing to the believers at Corinth, encourages both differences and variety. That is a challenge to us at times. Encouraging, achieving, and valuing variety and diversity is hard for us.

There is an old joke usually told around synod assembly time that goes something like this: Pastors are like manure. You get a big pile of them in one place and it can really stink, but if you spread them around they do pretty good work.

There is a degree of truth to this, in part because of something Paul suggests in this passage. We need variety in our gatherings. We need differences. Pastors are hardly identical, but they do tend to share similar gifts. In the same way we need diversity in our congregations.

What about the stranger in your midst? Perhaps the first thing we do when we encounter a new person is look to see if they are like us. Do they look the same? Do they wear similar clothes? Do they talk and think like we do? Do they seem to have the same values and perspective? There are more questions, and usually we go through a set of them trying to get an understanding of this new person. All of our questions lead to answering one basic one: Is this stranger like us?

Paul says the opposite is true of the people of God. We are to look to each other hoping we will be different. Not only are we to be different, but we should even celebrate the differences. Paul tells us this is for the good of the community we call the church. Variety in the people of God is expected, encouraged, and celebrated. Without it, we are less than we can be as the church.

Without variety the very gifts of the Holy Spirit are not present in the church. Paul uses the marvelous metaphor of the body later in 1 Corinthians 12. He asks, "Are we all hands? Are we all feet or ears or eyes?" Without the variety and diversity of different people with different gifts the body is not complete. God calls us to welcome the stranger, the different person. Then the gifts of the Spirit are all represented.

The church needs servants who are daring and bold, ready to strike out on a new path. The church also needs calm voices of wisdom and caution. Each voice is a blessing to the group. The church constantly needs to innovate while remaining faithful to our Lutheran heritage.

When we set aside ego and the need to be right, differences can actually bring people together. When our relationship with God is first, then we can humbly listen to others. When we care more for our relationship with our sisters and brothers in Christ than in being right, we can faithfully listen to their concerns and ideas.

How do we live faithfully?

Encourage diversity in the church. Welcome the stranger, welcome different people. Remember that the church needs hands, eyes, ears, and more. Without variety, without an inclusive church, the body suffers.

To be called by God to serve as a council member means to create an atmosphere that allows for including the stranger. It means to make sure the stranger, the visitor, is welcomed and made to feel at home. It means to celebrate the uniqueness of your congregation and its members. It means to use your varied gifts to share the good news of Jesus Christ

---

Questions

1. How does your congregation encourage or discourage variety?

2. What do you do to welcome first-time visitors?

3. How do you identify spiritual gifts and encourage their use?

10

Called by God to Serve

Read 1 Peter 2:4-5, 9-10

[4]Come to him, a living stone, though rejected by mortals yet chosen and precious in God's sight, and [5]like living stones, let yourselves be built into a spiritual house, to be a holy priesthood, to offer spiritual sacrifices acceptable to God through Jesus Christ.

[9]But you are a chosen race, a royal priesthood, a holy nation, God's own people, in order that you may proclaim the mighty acts of him who called you out of darkness into his marvelous light.

[10]Once you were not a people, but now you are God's people; once you had not received mercy, but now you have received mercy.

Does ministry only belong to pastors or church professionals? Who is responsible for ministry in Christ's church? Some would say the hired help, whether that is a pastor, youth worker, musician, secretary, sexton, school director, or another on the payroll of the congregation, is wholly responsible for ministry. Peter suggests another answer. Peter suggests that it is the calling of all baptized believers to be the ministers of Christ's church.

No one would build a house on a weak foundation. If one did, in a short time, the house would begin to settle and everything would be uneven. Eventually the house would fall down because of the poor foundation.

What is your congregation's foundation? Do you build the ministry of the church on the sure foundation of Jesus Christ? Peter reminds us that the cornerstone is Christ himself (v. 6). Christ has called us to do ministry. You can trust that foundation. Your cornerstone, the keystone, is Christ.

Christ makes you a "royal priesthood." It is not your own activity, insight, or talent that makes you a priest; it is the call of Christ that makes you part of his holy priesthood. "Once you were not a people, but now you are God's people" (v. 10). This is the difference being called by Christ makes. It literally forms our identity.

This calling makes you different. Peter writes, "Beloved, I urge you as aliens and exiles" (v. 11). You are an "alien" and an "exile" not belonging to this world but belonging to the kingdom of God. Because you are baptized believers, you live in this world but belong to God.

There are a variety of reasons people choose to join a specific congregation. Some people choose a congregation because of denominational loyalty, others because of location. Some choose a congregation because of the worship schedule. Whatever the specific reason, most people choose a congregation based on what that congregation has to offer them. They consider their needs and compare what churches have to offer, and the visiting begins. They travel from place to place, testing worship, reading brochures, and checking friendliness levels. And they have it completely backwards.

A more faithful way to find a congregation would be to first consider your gifts and what you have to offer to the congregation and its community. The congregation that needs your gifts is very likely the one you are called to join. This is the place God is sending you to serve.

If this sounds more like the path of a pastor than a layperson, this is because when we read these words from 1 Peter we often stop after the first meaning of the title, "royal priesthood." As Lutherans, we know this means that both lay people and pastors alike have equal access to God. Layperson or pastor, bishop or child, all our prayers come before God equally. We live this truth in worship when lay people serve as assisting ministers and lectors. We live this truth in daily life when we all pray for each other and when we visit the sick and lonely in Jesus' name.

But we must go beyond this first meaning of this grand title. All Christians are called to be servants, for that is the meaning of the word *priest*, one who serves the people of God. This means we all look to use our gifts in service to Christ first. We look for the good of the church and faithful living before ourselves.

Peter tells us to proclaim in our serving. "But you are a chosen race, a royal priesthood, a holy nation, God's own people, in order that you may proclaim the mighty acts of him who called you out of darkness into his marvelous light" (v. 9). This is how we serve, telling the mighty acts of God, especially in Jesus, through our words and deeds.

How do we live faithfully?

To be called by God to serve as a council member means that as a member of the priesthood of all believers, you too are called by God to serve God by serving others. You are called to use your gifts faithfully in service of God. As is often proclaimed at the end of worship: "Go in peace. Serve the Lord. Thanks be to God!" It is then that the real "service" begins.

Questions

1. How is your congregation a serving priesthood?

2. How does your congregation provide opportunities for every member to serve?

3. How does your congregation balance the focus of serving with a focus on Christ?

Year Two
Planning for Mission

Over the next several months, the authors hope the stories, questions, and reflections will spark good thinking and discussion. As you talk together and confront difficult issues from the safety of a story, it is the authors' prayer that you will be better prepared and less anxious when faced with similar events in the life of your parish.

Faithful leadership is a difficult calling. Leaders are called to have patience and hold to a larger, long-term vision. Leaders are asked to provide wisdom and guidance rather than give in to the tyranny of the crisis of the month. Many congregations have a mission statement—a plan for the future—that provides stability and direction. It is certainly true that if you do not know where you are going you will never know when you get there. As part of that plan for the future, the church budget reveals much about what is valued and what is not. Look at your congregation's budget and determine if the budget accurately reflects where the congregation is going and who you want to serve.

Leaders are called on to make decisions for the good of the church that not everyone agrees with. When necessary, faithful leaders will tolerate pain in themselves for the good of the congregation.

Leaders of the congregation set the tone. With an attitude of grace and generosity, the congregation is open to exciting possibilities. Forgiveness rather than blame allows creativity to flourish. Freed from the anxiety of sin, we can respond with creativity and hope.

Your faithful leadership is a gift to the church. By working through these reflections each month, you can monitor many difficult situations at a safe distance. As similar situations arise in the life of your congregation, remember your calm and thoughtful conversations during the past year. May God grant you honest and peaceful conversations and faithfulness in all things.

11

Focus on Mission

Read Philippians 3:12-14; Matthew 28:19-20
They are an average family, living in a modest home. One Saturday they went out for a drive and decided to make it a vacation. So they kept driving and went to some interesting places. They enjoyed themselves and considered it a good vacation. Unlike most folks, they did not pack before, nor did they think about where they wanted to go. They just piled everyone in the family car and drove off on vacation.

Most people do not vacation this way. Most know their destination, plan the trip, make reservations in advance, and so forth. Rare are the folks who would just get in the car, drive off, return in a week, and call it vacation.

The opposite is true of churches. Most congregations simply exist from week to week, not planning or having an idea of where they are going. The idea of setting goals does not occur to members. Rather, the typical church is just trying to survive. This is a significant problem for a number of reasons. Without a direction—a clear statement of mission—a congregation just flounders. With no particular place or destination in mind, members of the congregation have no idea where things are going. When a clear mission direction is missing, it affects the interaction of people and members tend to disagree among themselves.

Often this lack of planning and direction translates into an attitude of survival rather than of mission. All the energy and effort of the congregation becomes focused on staying alive. The message to visitors is one of panic or sometimes a closed door. Thus the congregation that lives out its unspoken goal—survival—eventually closes anyway.

What does this mean for your congregation? The church is called to mission. In his commission to the disciples, our Lord Jesus said, "Go therefore and make disciples of all nations" (v. 19). Jesus tells us that survival should not drive us as believers. Rather, we are called to be engaged in mission, seeking the lost and inviting them to become part of the Christian community, our congregation.

A mission statement will help your congregation stay focused on its mission. A mission statement must be short enough to be memorable. A mission statement is a timeless statement. If the mission is a reminder that could serve most congregations, that is fine. In a broad way, the call of the gospel is the same for all people.

Once you have a mission statement, you will need a series of goals. The goals move you from the general nature of a mission statement to the details of your specific setting. These goals describe how you will fulfill your mission statement. The goals should be updated and evaluated each year. They must be specific enough to aid in evaluating the past year and help in planning for the years to come.

Questions

1. What is your mission statement? Do you have one?

2. How has your mission guided your decisions as a church council?

3. How do you set goals?

4. How do you plan for the coming year, five years, and ten years?

12

What Do You Manage?

"You know, Chin and John have only worked here a few months," said Dean. "I don't see any reason why we should have to give them raises."

"But the suggested raise really isn't that much," responded Carol. "We would hardly even notice it in this budget."

The finance committee was meeting for its annual budget planning session. Things went smoothly until the salaries for two staff members came into consideration.

"If we give people raises every year they'll start expecting it no matter how hard they work," replied Dean as the conversation continued.

"How are we going to keep good people around if we don't pay them well?" asked Carol.

After much discussion Dean relented. "If the rest of the committee agrees with Carol, then fine, just give them the raises."

Ten minutes later the committee began to consider the electric bill. The previous winter had been very cold and costs exceeded the budgeted amount. The committee quickly added $1,000 to the utilities budget line.

Then they began discussing Sam's suggestion that they build a $10,000 surplus into the budget to deal with any contingencies during the year. The committee chose to limit the surplus to $5,000. The rest of the budget was soon completed and they went home satisfied.

Choose one or more of the questions below to assist your discussion. Discuss these questions before you continue with "Putting it together."

Questions

How does your annual budget reflect your care for people? What percent of your budget goes beyond the walls of your building?

In what ways is your congregation tempted to do as little as
   necessary to get by?

What does your budget reveal about the mission of the congregation?
   How willing are you to spend money on witnessing?

Putting it together
Read Matthew 10:5-7

> [5]These twelve Jesus sent out with the following instructions: "Go
> nowhere among the Gentiles, and enter no town of the
> Samaritans, [6]but go rather to the lost sheep of the house of Israel.
> [7]As you go, proclaim the good news, 'The kingdom of heaven has
> come near.'"

As leaders of the congregation, you are charged with the responsibility of caring for the church's finances. While this is important, it
is tempting to get stuck there. The mission of the congregation is
greater than the money. The mission is a holy calling from God.
Money is no more and no less than one of the many tools we might
use as we respond to God's call. The time and talent of members is
needed as well as money. They are also tools for mission and gifts
given by stewards.

   Jesus sent out the disciples to proclaim the good news of God's
kingdom. Just as he sent out the twelve, he sends us out as well, for
sent ones is our identity as believers. All Christians are called to be
witnesses. The church is a collection of people sent out into the
world to serve Christ.

   We serve Christ through acts of charity and mercy. We serve
Christ through faithfully giving of our financial resources. This is
called "proportional giving." We set aside from the beginning a part
of our wealth for God. The traditional tithe is 10 percent. Some set
aside less than 10 percent; others set aside more. What is important

is that the proportional gift is given first, in thanksgiving to God. As you do this you discover living on 90 percent is a joy and delight for you. You do not feel guilty, you know you are giving your gift, your proportional gift, and such a first fruit gift is pleasing to God.

We serve Christ by crafting a budget that reflects care for the people of the church and a desire to serve. Budgets become much more than a spending plan, they also reveal of our priorities as a congregation. Look closely at your budget, and it will tell you clearly how much you serve yourselves and how much you serve others.

13

How We Act as Leaders

Read Exodus 6:7-8

⁷I will take you as my people, and I will be your God. You shall
know that I am the Lord your God, who has freed you from the
burdens of the Egyptians. ⁸I will bring you into the land that I
swore to give to Abraham, Isaac, and Jacob; I will give it to you
for a possession. I am the Lord.'"

Faithful leadership is not easy. Gossip, manipulation, lies, and ultimatums pose difficulties in every congregation at one time or another.

It is tempting to focus on problems, taking them one at a time and offering a bag of tricks to deal with each in turn. Instead of focusing on problems, consider four characteristics essential for faithful leadership: vision, patience, centering, and responsibility.

A vision provides a goal, gives leaders a perspective, and allows leaders to evaluate suggestions. You will begin to ask how specific issues such as paving the parking lot, starting a preschool, or offering a second worship service fit with the congregation's vision for the future. A vision for the future will provide something positive to point toward.

This vision must be more than a human construction. In Exodus 6:7-8, God offers a clear vision for the future of the Israelites. God claims the people and promises them a hopeful future. It is no different now. God claims us and promises us a future. God's promise is general—and specific—in the same way God made the promise to the Israelites when they left Egypt.

Still, the promised land was farther off than the Israelites ever imagined. Even Moses, their leader, would not live to see them enter Canaan. With a strong vision for the future, a faithful leader needs patience, waiting for tensions to ease and progress to come in God's time.

Patience reduces reactivity. Patience provides the time and space for creativity to flourish and a wide variety of options to be considered. Patience will allow the faithful leader to persevere while holding fast to the long-term vision.

In order to have vision and patience, it is necessary to center our lives outside of ourselves. You need to know the perspective from which you lead. Jesus Christ as the revealed Word of God is the center of our life together. All of life is centered in our identity as children of God, loved and forgiven.

From this center, we can wait upon the future. Meanwhile, we take responsibility for ourselves and our mission. When we center in Christ, he calls us to serve others in his name, using our gifts and talents for others.

Centering and being responsible help us to avoid simply being led about by the whims of others. Sometimes you are asked to do things that do not fit the mission of your congregation. Your vision is the measure by which you decide if something fits and needs to be done.

The faithful leader is one who continually points to God's vision for the congregation while remaining patient in the face of anxiety and tension. The faithful leader centers in Jesus Christ and responds to the grace of God with obedience that acts responsibly.

Questions

1. What is God's vision for your congregation, and how do you share this vision?

2. How can you nurture patience in yourself?

3. What do you do daily to center yourself in Jesus Christ?

4. How are you taking responsibility for yourself and the mission of your congregation?

14

Faithful Leadership Hurts

Have you ever seen a teenager pout? If you failed to look into the mirror when you were a teen, you may, as an adult, have reason to see a teenager in full pout.

Alex certainly had the look. It was the end of the Sunday night youth meeting and he had just asked if he could give a ride home to his friend and fellow church member, Juan. Those who were the adult sponsors for the youth knew that wasn't possible. They had to say no. Alex was not happy. He was hurt because he felt the adult leaders didn't trust him or his driving. They tried their best to explain that it was church policy. Only adults over twenty-one years old could give rides. However, Alex at age sixteen and with a new driver's license, left that evening scowling and mad and most of the adults were upset and feeling like ogres.

What Alex did not know was the policy had been set in place more than thirty years before because of a terrible car accident. It was a hot summer Sunday afternoon and everyone in the youth group wanted to go to the lake to swim. One of the youth loaded his car with his friends from the church. It was a long drive, almost an hour. All went well until the last few minutes. The story becomes hazy at this point and the youth were not quite sure about what happened. Perhaps it was the gravel on the road. The car turned over and a sixteen-year-old boy was killed.

From this tragedy the church council voted unanimously to set the policy. Only adults would be driving youth to events and home. Transportation for youth would be by adults only.

Over the years, youth frequently complained. They felt they were being punished and picked on by the adults. It was not a pleasant discussion whenever it came up. Sometimes it is hard to enforce a policy that seems to pick on a person or a group in the congregation. Being a leader can hurt.

Choose one or more of the questions below to assist your discussion. Discuss these questions before you continue with "Putting it together."

Questions

1. When have you had to make decisions that you knew would cause controversy in the congregation?

2. How did you deal with the pain for all involved?

3. What helps you or hinders you from tolerating pain in yourself and others?

4. How would your council respond to the transportation situation described above?

Putting it together

Read Matthew 19:16-22

[16]Then someone came to him and said, "Teacher, what good deed must I do to have eternal life?" [17]And he said to him, "Why do you ask me about what is good? There is only one who is good. If you wish to enter into life, keep the commandments." [18]He said to him, "Which ones?" And Jesus said, "You shall not murder; You shall not commit adultery; You shall not steal; You shall not bear false witness; [19]Honor your father and mother; also, You shall love your neighbor as yourself." [20]The young man said to him, "I have kept all these; what do I still lack?" [21]Jesus said to him, "If you wish to be perfect, go, sell your possessions, and give the money to the poor, and you will have treasure in heaven; then come, follow me." [22]When the young man heard this word, he went away grieving, for he had many possessions.

Most of the decisions church councils make go unnoticed. But every so often, leaders are called by God to make decisions in the life of the congregation that will not please everyone. Some decisions might even cause hurt feelings and pain in the life of the congregation. One common first reaction to this is to give in. Regardless of right or wrong, we want to appease the hurt person, calm them down, and restore peace and harmony. This comes at a price, usually far greater than we initially realize.

Faithful leaders must have a tolerance for pain in themselves and in others. Rather than allow fear of others' reaction to control their decisions, they choose to act for the good of the church and for the protection of everyone.

We do not always like the truth when we hear it. We do not always like the truth when we have to speak it, but this is the calling of the faithful leader. When the young man came to Jesus seeking the way to eternal life, he did not want difficult tasks and expectations placed before him. When Jesus spoke the hard truth of the gospel to the young man, Jesus certainly did not want the man to walk away grieving. This is part of the pain of leadership.

Leaders who refuse to tolerate pain in themselves or others will find themselves blown about by every breeze that puffs up. As leaders of God's people, you are called to seek God's holy will and lead your congregation into the pathway of righteousness. There is sometimes a price to pay, but in the long run the road is indeed easier.

15

What Makes Us Strong?

Worthy Is Christ

This is the feast of victory for our God, Alleluia.
Worthy is Christ, the Lamb who was slain,
whose blood set us free to be people of God.
Power, riches, wisdom, and strength,
and honor, blessing, and glory are his.
Sing with all the people of God,
and join in the hymn of all creation.
Blessing, honor, glory, and might be to God and the Lamb forever.
Amen.
For the Lamb who was slain has begun his reign.
Alleluia.

Lutheran Book of Worship, pp. 60-61

We sing these familiar words on many Sundays in the Hymn of Praise from *Lutheran Book of Worship*. Council members certainly know the victory we sing about is far from complete. All congregations face conflicts and struggles that might shock new council members.

We may sing of the feast of victory, but we know in our lives, in the church, and in the world that the victory is both now and not yet. Sin still captures us in its deadly grip, destroying lives, relationships, and even nations and peoples. Looking at the world as it is, human beings as they are and the church as it is, we feel that we cannot sing about God's victory. Try as we might we will not find refuge in some glory days in the past. We are not any worse than we ever were.

It is only through eyes of faith that we see a hopeful future. Without faith in God's sustaining mercy, we are left to judge by the cynical values of the world. We jump from one quick fix to the next, bolstering the youth program one month and starting a contemporary worship service the next, trying to fix whatever appears to be the problem of the moment.

When the Israelites left Egypt, they were alone and frightened. The desert was an inhospitable and dangerous place. Food and water were scarce. But Moses trusted in God's promise to bring them to that land flowing with milk and honey. For forty years they wandered in the desert. Along the way they saw signs of God's mercy—the deliverance through the Red Sea, the gift of water at Elim and Rephidim, and the gift of manna in the wilderness of sin.

After forty years, God's promise was fulfilled but Moses and those who crossed the Red Sea died before Israel arrived in Canaan. When we look with hope to the future, we may find ourselves in Moses' shoes—traveling towards a great future that will only come after we have died.

As congregations, we learn about God and ourselves; we mourn as people and programs die; we are always recipients of God's grace. All of these experiences point us into the future. Just as the people of Israel wandered in the wilderness and looked to the future land, we travel knowing we have a place at Christ's kingdom table.

We travel forward together. We remember the past, but we remember forgiveness and grace all the more. We grieve, but not without hope for the future and confidence in God's mercy. We teach the faith to generations of children and adults so all people can come to trust in God's promises.

We are people of Baptism. In the Small Catechism, Martin Luther reminds us that Baptism "signifies that the old person in us with all sins and evil desires is to be drowned through daily sorrow for sin and repentance, and that daily a new person is to come forth and rise up to live before God in righteousness and purity forever." Baptism gives our future hope by God's promise of forgiveness.

As a council member, pray for God to grant you the courage to trust in God's future. Trust, even though you may never see it fully. Trust, even though you may be like Moses standing on the brink of the promised land. Plan with confidence and trust the Holy Spirit to guide your feet into the path of faith.

Questions

1. How does your congregation look with eyes of faith towards the future?

2. Where does your congregation avoid the future?

3. How do you focus on weakness?

4. How does it feel to sing, "This is the feast of victory for our God, Alleluia"?

5. How does knowing our final destination at God's kingdom table influence our travel along the way?

16

Being Gracious People

Do you remember times when you were privileged to be present for a very unusual and exciting congregational meeting? You are probably laughing now, since most congregational meetings are predictable and not at all exciting. Sometimes, there are congregational meetings that are memorable.

The president of the congregation, Lucille, called the meeting to order. The members of People of Faith Church still sat in their pews; the worship service had just ended. Lucille introduced her guest, Kendra, a representative of the area refugee resettlement committee. Kendra took the microphone and said she was at People of Faith to talk about the possibility of the congregation sponsoring a refugee family. She mentioned several times that there was a family from Bosnia that could arrive on Thursday but their original sponsoring organization had to back out. The family needed a sponsor; without a sponsor, the family would stay in the refugee camp. It was a family of five—a mother and father, two adult children, and a granddaughter. But, Kendra said she knew that Thursday might be too soon for People of Faith to respond. She held up a picture of the family and said that the family had lived for thirty months in a railroad box car with several other families. She was hoping that People of Faith would find this family a sponsor so their planned flight and other arrangements would not need to be cancelled.

When the president of the congregation took the floor once again, things began to happen. One member said, "Why can't we sponsor this family—starting this Thursday?" And then he pledged $100 toward the $3,000 needed to sponsor the family. Other hands shot up. Immediately $1,200 was pledged by several families, a person offered to see medical care was provided, another said she would work on dental arrangements, another would check into the schools education, and more people of faith responded.

It was an amazing moment. It was a time full of grace and love. Sight unseen, this congregation had begun to love a refugee family. You could tangibly feel the presence of God's Holy Spirit challenging and encouraging the congregation. It was a special time. The sponsorship would go well and the family would become self-supporting quickly and buy a home within two years. It was a gracious moment. It was a gracious experience for the gathered people of God.

Choose one or more of the questions below to assist your discussion. Discuss these questions before you continue with "Putting it together."

Questions

1. When have you had congregational meetings that you would consider to be gracious moments for your church?

2. How can you have more gracious moments in your congregation? Can gracious moments be created, or must they happen spontaneously?

3. What key elements are needed for members to treat each other gracefully?

4. How does treating others well outside the congregation encourage members to treat one another well?

Putting it together

Read Matthew 25:34-36

[34]Then the king will say to those at his right hand, 'Come, you that are blessed by my Father, inherit the kingdom prepared for you from the foundation of the world; [35]for I was hungry and you gave me food, I was thirsty and you gave me something to drink,

I was a stranger and you welcomed me, [36]I was naked and you gave me clothing, I was sick and you took care of me, I was in prison and you visited me.'"

As a leader, you are in a key position to influence gracious actions by others. How you interact with others will send a message of how we are to treat one another. Modeling gracious care of others encourages everyone to do the same.

Gracious living requires that we know ourselves and what is expected of us. If you are the congregational president, then you hold the primary office of the elected leadership. You are responsible to see that the congregation is administered well: that financial and property matters are handled appropriately; that long-range planning is done and accomplished; and finally, to see that appropriate nominees are presented to the congregation for future leadership positions. This brief job description of the responsibilities of a president tells you what it is you are to be doing and not doing. You can define your role clearly: planning is yours, preaching belongs to the pastor. Cleaning the building is the janitor's responsibility, seeing that an annual audit is done is yours. So it goes.

Along with defining ourselves well we need to have clear goals and tasks that all have agreed are best for the congregation. Then everyone can work toward them. Contributing to and meeting mutual goals with one another leads to gracious living.

Most of all, as our Lord says above, when we are about caring for those who are poor we are serving at our best. Gracious living seeks out those who are lost, last, and least. We express grace and love in relationship with these folks. When we serve the refugee we are most at home with God.

17

On Not Being Ourselves

Read Luke 12:2-3

> [Jesus said,] ²"Nothing is covered up that will not be uncovered, and nothing secret that will not become known. ³Therefore whatever you have said in the dark will be heard in the light, and what you have whispered behind closed doors will be proclaimed from the housetops."

We expect schools to be safe places for children to learn. When violence erupts in a school, the shock is overwhelming. We wonder how such a horrible thing could happen there.

Families are expected to be places of love and happiness. Most families work hard to project an image of happiness to the world. When homes are torn apart by anger, violence, or divorce, the foundation of our lives is shaken.

Similarly, churches are expected to be places of peace, free from conflict. When conflict and anger appear, people will often remark, "I cannot believe this is happening in a church." Or you may hear, "Churches should not be like this."

As in schools and homes, the reality of sin causes pain and damage in churches. Ignoring the problems will not make them disappear. Ignoring problems will only make them worse. Our Lord Jesus addresses this with these startling words: "Nothing is covered up that will not be uncovered, and nothing secret that will not become known" (Luke 12:2-3).

All our secrets will be revealed. The truth can be painful, but truth also brings healing. Conflict ignored and denied will grow. Gossip will spread like a weed if allowed. Untruthful statements and manipulation can ruin the church if left alone in the dark to grow.

The gospel light shines into the deepest darkness of our lives. The gospel light pierces the gloom of our denial with words of truth. In his prayer, our Lord calls us to forgive one another as we ourselves have been forgiven. When we practice forgiveness, our lives are free in a whole new way. Now we can risk challenging people—we can risk speaking out in truth and honesty—because we can trust in the mercy of God coming to us through one another to forgive us.

Forgiveness begins with confession. We confess that we are sinners and are in need of the grace of God that will forgive us. Only as we faithfully seek God's forgiveness and know we are given it in the cross of Christ can we then forgive one another. Our acts of forgiving grow from the forgiveness of God. It is grace bearing love in us.

Two particular things happen when we acknowledge our sin and know God's forgiveness. First, we become much more flexible people. Knowing that we are recipients of grace makes us open to others, listening, seeking to understand, that we might be gracious with them as well. Being flexible and open listeners is part of the gift of forgiveness, and these are signs of the presence of forgiveness in our lives.

The second result of being forgiven is greater creativity. When we live in the grace of God, we are far less anxious and are able to respond to challenges and issues with superior creativity. Anxiety binds and limits us, forgiveness and grace set us free to be the best we are as the people of God.

Questions

1. Where is darkness hiding conflict?

2. How can you practice forgiveness among council members?

3. How can you practice forgiveness as a congregation?

4. When have you been flexible and creative as a council? What difference did this make?

18

Speaking the Truth in Love

To build or not to build was the question. The meeting room table was an old, round kitchen table, but it was long and sturdy. Eleven council members and the pastor sat around it. Discussion followed after an exercise in estimating the capacity of the congregation to support the cost of the proposed building project. Two of the men spoke up about their fears: "If we do this the congregation will go bankrupt and it will close." Others gave their perspective. Everyone spoke. A vote was taken and the majority voted in favor of building.

It was outside, on the sidewalk, when Ozzie spoke again with Paul: "I just don't think we can afford it, Paul, and I am surprised you did not vote with John and me against building." "You know, Ozzie, I really feel like you do, but I can't disappoint the pastor, and he really seems to be in favor it." Ten or fifteen minutes of conversation went by. Ozzie and Paul decided to call some other members of the council the next day to see if they could vote again. Maybe they could get the project voted down.

The meeting after the meeting had a more honest exchange. Speaking the truth in love can be challenging. It is not helpful to hold back the truth until the sidewalk or the parking lot after the meeting. As a congregation council member, how do you respond to meetings after the meeting?

Choose one or more of the questions below to assist your discussion. Discuss these questions before you continue with "Putting it together."

Questions

1. When you have experienced this kind of situation? How did you feel about it?

2. In what ways does the behavior of Ozzie and Paul undermine the leadership in the congregation?

3. How might the congregation council encourage open and honest dialog in its meetings?

4. What might you say to speak the truth in love to members of the congregation council who hold meetings after the meeting?

5. What roadblocks operate in your meetings now that keep open and honest conversation from taking place?

Putting it together

Read Ephesians 4:14-16

[14]We must no longer be children, tossed to and fro and blown about by every wind of doctrine, by people's trickery, by their craftiness in deceitful scheming. [15]But speaking the truth in love, we must grow up in every way into him who is the head, into Christ, [16]from whom the whole body, joined and knit together by every ligament with which it is equipped, as each part is working properly, promotes the body's growth in building itself up in love.

Clearly, meetings that discourage open and honest conversation do not support faithful leadership. Similarly, people who refuse to be open and honest during a meeting and then complain later are being destructive. Confronting people we love and care for is not easy. Complaining about the frustration of the "meetings after the meeting" while never confronting the other person is often our chosen response. This behavior, however, does not build up the body of Christ.

True Christian love of our brothers and sisters calls us to walk the difficult path of honesty and openness. We do not do this for ourselves. We do it for the good of the whole body of Christ. In all of life we benefit from others who love us enough to point out our blind spots and remind us of our transgressions. Thanks be to God for our friends who love us enough to confront us.

To confront someone means to deal with them directly and honestly. Confrontation does not mean that we have to be nasty or verbally assault the person. We can speak the truth in love. This is particularly true for those who follow Jesus as their Lord. Called to love one another, we must speak openly and honestly with one another and not in a nasty or assaulting manner. Sometimes the best approach is a question or two. However you choose to say it, be kind in the process as well as in the content as you speak the truth in love.

19

Your Mind
and the Mind of Christ

Read Philippians 2:3-5

> [3]Do nothing from selfish ambition or conceit, but in humility
> regard others as better than yourselves. [4]Let each of you look not
> to your own interests, but to the interests of others. [5]Let the same
> mind be in you that was in Christ Jesus.

The advertising slogan of a fast-food company said: "You deserve a
break today!" Do you?

We live in a world that surrounds us with images urging us to
consider ourselves first. Advertisements frequently lure people to
buy the product by promising great advantages to individuals,
regardless of hidden costs others might bear. In all things, we are
encouraged to take care of ourselves. We listen to these voices, to the
exclusion of voices like the apostle Paul, because they tell us exactly
what we want to hear.

It has been said that all sin can be reduced to breaking the first
commandment: "You shall have no other gods." The most common
way of violating the first commandment is by worshiping one's self:
Take care of yourself first. Do all things from selfish ambition. Look
to your own interests.

This is so deeply a part of the human experience that even the
television comedy *Friends*, featured an episode in which two of the
characters came to the conclusion that there can be no wholly self-
less act. Even at our most faithful, we place our needs, desires, and
security ahead of others.

We can see this in congregations. When there is a hymn you do
not like, what do you do? Do you keep silent, pretend to sing, or sing

as well as you can to support the singing of your sisters and brothers who may like the hymn? Too frequently, divisions in churches arise from small, even petty, differences. Why is the exact shade of white paint so important in the new fellowship hall? Why does the color of the carpet matter so much?

When your focus is on taking care of your own, you will do just that, and most likely little else. How would your church appear to someone the first time they visited? Can they locate parking and bathrooms easily? Do people help them follow the worship order? Are newcomers made to feel welcome?

Churches are good at maintaining buildings. Churches are good at feeding themselves at covered-dish dinners. Is your congregation as good at providing shelter for those living in poverty? Is your congregation as good at feeding those who are hungry? How about clothing those who are naked? How do you care for those who are lost, last, and least?

We proclaim the good news of Jesus Christ through preaching God's word and sharing the sacraments. We also proclaim the good news of Jesus Christ by feeding those who hungry and caring for those who are poor. If the good news does not lead you out, away from concerns for yourself, and turn your eyes to the interests of others, the gospel has yet to capture you.

This is not simply a reminder of the importance of social ministry committees. This is a call to all members of the congregation to lift their eyes and behold God's great vision of a gathered people sharing a great feast. This is God's vision of people caring for one another in an interconnected web of love and service that includes all people.

The call to focus on the needs of others first is essential for all human relationships. This call has implications for all aspects of our lives.

Questions

1. In what ways do you as a church council fulfill the first commandment?

2. How does your congregation determine which needs—internal vs. external—get priority?

20

Who Do You Say That I Am?

"Well, we now have a plumber-pastor," announced Chuck at the meeting. He was referring to the fact that Pastor Neil, the new pastor, had repaired the leaky toilet valve in the pastor's restroom that is adjacent to his office.

On his very first day in the office, Pastor Neil became aware of the sound of dripping water. He did a bit of detective work and discovered the valve was leaking in the tank—and the leak was more than a drip, drip. Water was constantly running, wasting many gallons of water each day. He called Chuck, the chairperson of the property committee, to get someone to repair the toilet. Sitting at his desk and listening to the water run continuously really bothered him. It was so wasteful.

Over the course of the next two weeks, Pastor Neil talked to Chuck about the leaky toilet valve. Finally, out of frustration, Pastor Neil fixed it himself and at his own expense. It took him just under two hours one Saturday afternoon and cost less than $10.00.

On Sunday, when Chuck found out about the repair, he started calling Pastor Neil, "Plumber-Pastor." Chuck thought it was great that the congregation had not only called a pastor but also a capable handyman. He kidded Pastor Neil that he had a long list of little projects around the church that needed to be taken care of by someone. The trouble was, Neil was not certain that Chuck was kidding.

Choose one or more of the questions below to assist your discussion. Discuss these questions before you continue with "Putting it together."

Questions

1. In the story about the broken toilet valve, how did the pastor and the property committee chairperson contribute to the problem?

2. Whose responsibility is it to evaluate the pastor's time and talent?

3. Are there clearly defined roles for the pastor and leaders of your congregation that are agreed upon by all?

4. Are the responsibilities of all paid employees written down and filed in the church office?

5. What process might be used to clarify the responsibilities of the pastor and leaders?

Putting it together

Read Matthew 16:13-16

[13]Now when Jesus came into the district of Caesarea Philippi, he asked his disciples, "Who do people say that the Son of Man is?" [14]And they said, "Some say John the Baptist, but others Elijah, and still others Jeremiah or one of the prophets." [15]He said to them, "But who do you say that I am?" [16]Simon Peter answered, "You are the Messiah, the Son of the living God."

When there is not a clear understanding of the role of the pastor, the congregational president, other leaders, paid employees, and volunteers, it is hard for the mission and ministry of the congregation to be done. Confused roles or an incomplete definition of tasks leads to chaos. Everyone assumes they know what the pastor and others are to be doing but, too often, what results is an unrealistic list of expectations. Very little gets accomplished. When the property committee does not take care of a plumbing problem and the pastor does, other tasks such as visitation, sermon preparation, and other work may not happen. When roles aren't clear, confusion, resentment, and exhaustion are likely to set in.

Even Jesus took time near Caesarea Philippi to pause and clarify who he was for his disciples. He asked, "Who do the people say that I am?" Several incomplete answers were given. Then he asked the disciples, "Who do you say that I am?" And Peter responded, "You are the Messiah, the Son of the living God."

This was not the end of the story. Jesus defined what it means to be the Messiah in a manner that Peter and the others did not expect, welcome, or understand. Jesus knew that to be the Messiah would bring a journey to the cross. Our mission requires that we are clear about how we define ourselves.

Thus, one of the most important activities of leadership is to define roles clearly. The pastor and leaders together need to agree upon what their duties are. When they agree, these duties are then communicated to the congregation. Once leaders have communicated expectations to all, it is their responsibility to faithfully and consistently carry out those duties.

Equally, leaders need to define their roles to the congregation so that members know with whom to speak regarding matters of concern. If there is a plumbing problem, don't go to the pastor or the treasurer, seek out the property committee. When roles are clear, the pastor, president, committees, and others are set free to do what is their work and not to have to worry about and do the work of others.

Year Three

Facing Difficult Challenges

This year's reflections place before you many difficult challenges and issues. You may have already addressed some, some will happen to you, and others may never arise in your congregation. But you know the feeling when one of these tough issues comes along.

The twenty-first century is a time of fast change in the world. Technology is constantly changing and updating. Children seem to get older younger. Many things people have assumed are being brought into question. Add to this the stresses congregations experience as denominations face decline and financial difficulties ensue. It is no surprise that churches are places where people feel that they can vent their anxieties. It is safe in the church in a way it may not be safe at home, school, or work.

As a leader in the church your job will not get easier. Now more than ever, your calm focus on the future is called for. Now more than ever, the church needs faithful leaders who are responsive to the needs of the people. Now more than ever, the church needs leaders who faithfully model the gospel.

As a leader in the church, you have a holy calling from God to serve. Through the issues you will face, you will change. You will see the church from a different perspective. You will be a different person. The greatest gift you can give your congregation is that of faithful serving. As you have responded to the reflections in this book it is the authors' prayer that you have grown in your understanding of God's call and are better prepared for what the future holds.

21

Hospitality

Read Hebrews 13:1-2

[1]Let mutual love continue. [2]Do not neglect to show hospitality to strangers, for by doing that some have entertained angels without knowing it.

One Sunday morning, the parents of two teenagers—a brother and sister—were serving as ushers. The boy and girl would have to sit alone in church. Breanne was feeling her radical teenage spirit and suggested that they enter the nave by the far right door and sit there. Their family had never done this. They always entered by the far left door and sat in one of the first rows on that side.

The two teenagers were daring. They entered the sanctuary, took two steps inside, looked at each other, and turned around and headed straight for the far left door. They knew the church building inside and out. Still, there was something about the other side of the nave that was too much for their teenage minds to cope with that morning. So they went back to "their side" and sat in "their pew" and talked with their friends.

It is not that we do not like to see new faces, but we get into our routine. We like a certain order to life. We do not always want to be bothered with other folks.

Our congregations are not filled with rude people, but we get comfortable where we are. We get comfortable in our favorite pew. It may be the back righthand corner or it may be the third row from the front, pulpit side. It makes no difference.

It is even more difficult when new people visit. How do you respond when they wear strange clothes? What do you do when their race is so noticeably different? Why is Sunday morning often called the most segregated time of the week in this country?

On the cross, Christ opened his arms to all. In the great commission (Matthew 28:19-20) our Lord Jesus sent us into all the world to proclaim the good news of the kingdom of God. Yet, even on Sunday morning, our habits and our need for comfort control us and overwhelm even Jesus' commission.

Hospitality can be an offering. Reaching out to the stranger and visitor can be like giving a gift to them. You look over one Sunday and see visitors who cannot find a worship book. You go to them and give it to them, opening to the right page. In so doing, you have made an offering that is a gift to these new worshipers in your congregation.

If your congregation distributes food to hungry people, do you invite them to share the Lord's Supper with you also? Our Lord calls us to care for all people. Yet our comfort levels usually urge us to invite those who drive cars similar to ours, dress as we do, talk as we do, and live as we do, and look like us.

As a council member, you are a leader. Be a model for your congregation. Sit in a different seat on Sunday morning. Meet some different people. Visit with folks you might not normally visit with next Sunday. Invite people who are different; they too are created in the image of God. Invite people who bring new personality and new gifts, that your congregation may more fully resemble the whole people of God in Christ Jesus.

Questions

1. In what ways is your Sunday morning routine determined by hospitality?

2. How might your congregation become more welcoming?

3. What is your congregation doing that deliberately invites and includes others?

22

Just a Complaint Department?

It was the second Monday of the month, and they met for yet another council meeting. This year the council had gotten into a painful rut. This month's meeting started just like last month's meeting and the month before and the month before that. No sooner had the pastor finished the prayer and the council added their "Amen," than Samantha piped up, "Someone has to teach those acolytes the proper way to do things. If they can't remember to light the candle on the right first, then maybe we need some new acolytes."

"We have bigger problems than that with worship," said Joan. "Mrs. Chen complained to me again this Sunday about not being able to hear. When are we going to get a decent public address system?"

"A new PA? We need a new refrigerator in the kitchen first. That old one is on its last legs. One of these mornings we will get to church, and there won't be a single cube of ice for the punch." Karl Weisbaum was visibly upset.

"At least the fridge is still working," said Greg. "That is more than I can say for this janitor. I practically have to clean the bathroom myself before I use it these days."

"I want to know who is choosing the hymns we are singing lately. None of them are familiar, and I hear a lot of people complaining," Grace whispered to Kathy at the end of the table. "Someone needs to do something about that, and soon."

"You know, I remember this time last year when we decided to get rid of that big ugly bush out in front of the church. Well, it's still out there, and in a week or two it will take over the whole sidewalk." Heads nodded in agreement and the complaining continued.

The council meeting lasted nearly three hours. Very little was decided. Many issues from the previous month had carried over as well, making the list longer still. When they finally adjourned, everyone left feeling tired and frustrated. Each person went home wondering as they drove: Why do the same issues arise month after month? Why is it that when one issue is resolved another replaces it?

Choose one or more of the questions below to assist your discussion. Discuss these questions before you continue with "Putting it together."

Questions

1. In what ways is the complaining of the church council familiar?

2. Why do you think congregations get into ruts like this?

3. What are the top three challenges for your congregation?

4. What goals might guide you as you take on these challenges?

5. What concrete tasks are needed to accomplish your goals?

Putting it together

Read Luke 15:28-32

[28]Then [the elder son] became angry and refused to go in. His father came out and began to plead with him. [29]But he answered his father, "Listen! For all these years I have been working like a slave for you, and I have never disobeyed your command; yet you have never given me even a young goat so that I might celebrate with my friends. [30]But when this son of yours came back, who has devoured your property with prostitutes, you killed the fatted calf for him!" [31]Then the father said to him, "Son, you are always with me, and all that is mine is yours. [32]But we had to celebrate and rejoice, because this brother of yours was dead and has come to life; he was lost and has been found."

When we focus on what is wrong and focus on relieving the pain of the moment, it is easy to forget the future. Today's problems are often more than enough for today and long-term planning is simply ignored. Unless people hold some greater vision for the congregation, they will tend to complain and pick apart what is happening.

The older brother in the parable of the prodigal son cannot see any future. He cannot join the joyous celebration of the return of his brother and delight with his father that the future will now be different. All the brother can do is to look to the past and complain. His father has to point out the grace-moment, that his brother who was lost is found. What a future they now have.

Long-term planning is not easy work. It often seems unrewarding and unhelpful. Still, it is essential for the health and vitality of God's people and their mission.

Imagine the joy and relief if the congregation's energy could be focused on accomplishing goals together. What a relief each month at the council meeting to hear an update of progress and challenges overcome or engaged, rather than a list of petty complaints. Now the church is freed for service to the living God. This is indeed who God calls us to be. We can join the celebration and delight in all that is happening.

23

In Dying We Live

Read Romans 6:1-5

[1]What then are we to say? Should we continue in sin in order that grace may abound? [2]By no means! How can we who died to sin go on living in it? [3]Do you not know that all of us who have been baptized into Christ Jesus were baptized into his death? [4]Therefore we have been buried with him by baptism into death, so that, just as Christ was raised from the dead by the glory of the Father, so we too might walk in newness of life. [5]For if we have been united with him in a death like his, we will certainly be united with him in a resurrection like his.

For her entire life, Alice had been a faithful member of her congregation. Through most of those years, Alice knew money was an issue for the congregation. In her lifetime, the congregation never had called a full-time pastor. They simply could not afford the cost; most of those years they shared a pastor with a congregation thirty miles away. As it happened, the two congregations rarely agreed on the pastor in question. It was a difficult situation.

Throughout Alice's lifetime there was an unspoken fear that her beloved church would one day run out of funds and members and be forced to close. Fear for her congregation motivated her to establish a trust fund in her will of $375,000 to keep the church going. Fear of dying held the congregation in bondage. Fear of death influenced decisions and held change in check.

How often does fear of congregational death caused by declining membership or the possibility of pain influence decisions? Sadly, this overwhelming fear reveals a lack of faith and trust in God.

God has promised that Christ's holy Church will exist to the end of all ages. That promise does not hold in the same way for individual congregations. When our faith is in God, no matter how deeply we love our own congregation, our vision must be broader.

Consider how the following example is a broader vision of the church: When a person is inactive in a congregation for more than six months, they are unlikely to return to that congregation. They are far more likely to return to worship at another congregation. What if neighboring congregations exchanged lists of inactive members? What a blessing it could be to the body of Christ and the church that more folks return to hear God's holy Word.

But if you fear the death of your congregation, why would you share those names with another congregation? After all, they are your members, aren't they?

The resurrection of Jesus Christ brings with it the promise of eternal life after death, and it also speaks to congregations and people in the midst of life. Death is destroyed, hell is crushed underfoot. Now, in faith, we can be courageous, boldly reaching out, motivated by our confident faith in Jesus Christ, not bound by the strangling fear of death.

In the resurrection we are not promised a return to some past greatness. Instead, God promises to open a great and glorious future before us. Life will not be the same. The old will pass away and the new will rise up in its place.

This news is at once fabulous and frightening. The future is beyond our control. When our vision is only a return to the past, a new future can be difficult to imagine and even harder to embrace. Still, we go forward, trusting in God to guide us through the power of the Holy Spirit. We place our faith in God's promise to raise us from the death and dust of this world, to the joy of a new creation.

It is in dying that we rise. Our faith calls us to look to the future with hope, trusting that God will continue to sustain the church.

Questions

1. What could happen if your congregation shared the names of inactive members with another neighboring congregation?

2. How can congregations be reborn from the ashes of failure, disappointment, or discord?

3. In what concrete ways can you share resurrection love with others in the future?

24

How Do We Grieve?

Katie was driving her friends in the drama club to a special event for all the local high schools. They were to perform their original one-act play for the assembled drama clubs. They were excited. It was a wonderful tribute to their hard work. They couldn't wait to get there.

She was driving too fast for the curve that took them under the highway. As she turned, the car began to slide. Suddenly, the car slammed into the bridge support, careened off the highway, and flipped over twice before stopping on its side. The four students riding with Mary all had their seatbelts on and walked away. But the left side of Katie's head had hit the window frame as it was crushed in on her by the impact. She died instantly. She was only seventeen.

Katie was baptized at Christ Church. She had been confirmed three years before the accident. Now her funeral would be there as well. Even though she was just in high school, she served regularly as an assisting minister at Sunday worship services. Everyone in the congregation knew her. They were stunned by her sudden and untimely death. Her parents and brother grieved openly, and everyone joined with them. The pain, sorrow, and sadness touched every member of the congregation.

Stunned and hurt, the church council struggled for ways to respond to the situation.

Choose one or more of the questions below to assist your discussion. Discuss these questions before you continue with "Putting it together."

Questions

1. How can a congregation go through a grieving process?

2. As leaders, how can you proclaim the good news of Christ's care for the congregation in their grief?

3. What are some of the losses your congregation has grieved or not grieved?

4. What prevents healthy grieving?

Putting it together

Read John 11:21-27

[21]Martha said to Jesus, "Lord, if you had been here, my brother would not have died. [22]But even now I know that God will give you whatever you ask of him." [23]Jesus said to her, "Your brother will rise again." [24]Martha said to him, "I know that he will rise again in the resurrection on the last day." [25]Jesus said to her, "I am the resurrection and the life. Those who believe in me, even though they die, will live, [26]and everyone who lives and believes in me will never die. Do you believe this?" [27]She said to him, "Yes, Lord, I believe that you are the Messiah, the Son of God, the one coming into the world."

All congregations suffer losses—from the sudden and tragic death of a young person to the expected but painful death of the faithful long-time member of the congregation. When a beloved pastor retires or leaves to take a new call after many years, there is a loss to grieve. When the congregation changes significantly over a short time, there are losses to grieve.

Like people, congregations can get stuck in their grief. When a congregation is stuck mourning the great pastor who many thought "never did anything wrong," the next several pastors come and go quickly, as each one fails to measure up. When we get stuck in grief, we go nowhere. This is doubly painful for Christians, as it reveals that we have forgotten the very foundation of the faith. We gather as people bound by sin, living with pain, suffering, and tragedy. God promises that we are redeemed from hopelessness by the cross of Christ.

In times of pain and grief, we may be tempted to turn away. But as leaders of the church you have the responsibility to call the people to faithfulness. You have a holy calling from God to find creative and daring ways to bring the power of the resurrection to bear on the pain and grief of the congregation. How this happens will depend on you, your congregation, your situation, and the Holy Spirit working in and through the people of God.

25

Right, Wrong, or Forgiven

Read Matthew 18:21-22

[21]Then Peter came and said to him, "Lord, if another member of the church sins against me, how often should I forgive? As many as seven times?" [22]Jesus said to him, "Not seven times, but, I tell you, seventy-seven times."

Kathara stared at the congregational president as he sat across the room explaining the action taken by the council at the last meeting. As he ended, she became furious. The council's action was not something she agreed with, and she felt strongly it should not have been taken by the council.

The conversation became quickly heated. Voices rose in pitch and volume. Then Kathara turned to the president and, stretching out her arm with index finger extended and shaking, she began, "If you ever do that again when I am not here, I will never forgive you."

The council was stunned into silence. The heated words seared an indelible mark on the meeting. "Never forgive you" are strong words, especially when they are said in anger and accusation. They are also words that conflict with the teaching of our Lord Jesus. He saw things differently.

To be in relationship with others means there will be pain. The church is a collection of sinners living together, so it is certain some toes will get stepped on by someone. Words will be spoken in anger. We are not always gracious and loving with one another.

God knows this better than we do. God knows relationships depend on forgiveness. If we are to be together we need to be forgivers. Knowing this, God forgives us from the beginning. On the cross on that lonely hilltop Jesus Christ stretches out his arms to forgive all.

We have a relationship with God because God so deeply desires it. We are forgiven our sins, our betrayals, our failures, and our destructiveness. We have a relationship with God only because God makes it possible.

In response to God's mercy we are called to forgive one another, to love one another with the love we know in Christ. This is not easy. Sometimes it means confessing our sins to one another. We forgive because God has forgiven us.

In Christ, we are called to forgive. Forgiving is not a matter of right or wrong. As leaders in the church we can disagree and hold strong positions that differ. We do not use the withholding of forgiveness as a threat to manipulate others.

Questions

1. Who are you called to forgive this day? Might it be someone here now?

2. How might you live out the forgiveness of God in this congregation council?

3. How does forgiveness make your congregation different from other organizations?

26

Spreading like Wildfire

When the phone rang, Mary left the kitchen and walked into the living room to answer it. Her sister had some wonderful news about a nephew. As they chatted, Mary suddenly realized there was smoke pouring out of the kitchen and gathering around the ceiling of the living room. Mary hung up the phone, dialed 911, and looked into the kitchen. The bacon she had been frying for her famous German potato salad had caught fire. She ran outside to wait for the fire department, already knowing there would be many disappointed folks at next Sunday's potluck supper when Mary's famous German potato salad failed to arrive.

The fire was quickly put out, thanks to Mary's phone call. While the house smelled like a campfire for the next several weeks it was livable—livable everywhere, that is, except the kitchen. What was not burned was coated with thick, gooey soot. The contractor promised to begin work soon, and then in only a few weeks, it would be done. Mary could only wait.

Meanwhile at the church, chaos set in. Mary had always baked all the communion bread. The first Sunday after the fire, Susan heard Joan say she would make the communion bread. Joan heard Susan promise to bake it. Neither did, so the tasteless wafers returned again. There were many complaints. The next Sunday, Mildred baked the bread, but she was new to bread-baking and her bread was tough and dry. Complaints arose again. And so it continued for several weeks.

When the annual congregation meeting arrived, there were more complaints. A motion was passed and the issue was referred to the worship committee, which was to draft a document explaining just how to prepare communion bread. This would then be passed on to the council and finally back to the congregation for their approval at a specially called meeting. All this started by a small grease fire.

Choose one or more of the questions below to assist your discussion. Discuss these questions before you continue with "Putting it together."

Questions

1. Identify the connections at work in the story. How is your congregation similar?

2. How has a change in one part of your congregation rippled throughout the congregation in unexpected ways?

3. How do you respond when something like this story happens in your congregation?

Putting it together

Read 1 Corinthians 12:24b-27

24bGod has so arranged the body, giving the greater honor to the inferior member, 25that there may be no dissension within the body, but the members may have the same care for one another. 26If one member suffers, all suffer together with it; if one member is honored, all rejoice together with it. 27Now you are the body of Christ and individually members of it.

Congregations are the sum of the connections and relationships between the members and the triune God. Because of these connections, change in one part brings change to another part. Therefore, it is not surprising that the change in communion bread preparation affected so many people. When planning for a change, expect unintended consequences. Changes will often have an effect far greater than just the change itself.

We are all connected to one another. This great blessing can also cause great turmoil. The apostle Paul explains this with the image of the human body. Paul tells us we are all part of the body of Christ. Our lives touch in such an intimate way that we all suffer together and we are all honored together. The church is more than a collection of individuals. The church is the body of Christ, alive and active in the world.

Some changes are out of our control. A faithful member dies or a storm floods the basement and the congregation changes in an instant. Other changes come as part of a plan for the future. An addition is built, a new parking lot is paved, or a contemporary worship service is added. No matter what the change is, not everyone will be happy.

As a leader, be alert to the words and actions of people around you. Note how they impact your words and actions. Find ways to be an island of calm even in the midst of a chaotic sea. Pray to God for patience and courage.

The connections we share with one another—and most significantly with God—are more important than anything else in the life of the congregation. The building does not matter. The time of worship does not matter. Relationships matter. Jesus said, "You shall love the Lord your God with all your heart and soul and mind and love your neighbor as yourself" (Luke 10:27). The rest will fall into place.

27

Faithful Leaders Challenge People

Luke 18:18-22

> [18]A certain ruler asked [Jesus], "Good Teacher, what must I do to inherit eternal life?" [19]Jesus said to him, "Why do you call me good? No one is good but God alone. [20]You know the commandments: 'You shall not commit adultery; You shall not murder; You shall not steal; You shall not bear false witness; Honor your father and mother.'" [21]He replied, "I have kept all these since my youth." [22]When Jesus heard this, he said to him, "There is still one thing lacking. Sell all that you own and distribute the money to the poor, and you will have treasure in heaven; then come, follow me."

The annual meeting was uneventful until Dale stood to give the report of the education committee. "We received an e-mail last week from the missionary the Sunday school children help sponsor in Tanzania. He wrote that their school and medical clinic had been nearly destroyed by fire. No one was seriously hurt and they were able to save a few items, but most everything else was gone." Dale looked at the faces of those at the meeting and continued speaking. "They need a minimum of $3,000 to start over." He stopped and sat down.

A full minute passed and the room was silent. Rhonda Meyers, the council president, was getting nervous and was about to stand and go to the next agenda item. Then Don and Florence stood up together, long-time, elderly members of the church. "We'll contribute $1,000," Don said. Everyone was shocked; they knew the Greiners didn't have much money. Then Harvey, who owned the hardware store, stood and donated $500. Dan Bald Eagle, a physician, said, "Here's my check for $800, and I'm sure the hospital will donate some unused medical equipment." Then others stood, each calling out the amount they wanted to contribute. By the end of the meeting, over $6,000 was raised with plans for ten people to travel to Tanzania as soon as possible to help rebuild.

This would not have happened had leaders not been willing to challenge the members of the congregation. You could feel the Holy Spirit moving through the assembly. It was like the room was on fire with love and commitment. What a gift for everyone, let alone the people who depended on the school and clinic. It all happened because of leaders willing to challenge others.

As leaders, we do people a disservice when we ask as little of them as possible. Faithful leaders will challenge people in a variety of ways. We all need to be challenged to grow in faith, to grow in understanding, to grow in service, and to grow in stewardship. Often leaders give in to temptation and ask too little of people rather than too much. Instead of spreading the responsibilities around, we take care of them ourselves or ask the same few people who we know will say yes. Without challenges, people do not grow. Without opportunities, people do not serve.

Christ's holy church needs strong, faithful leaders who hold high expectations for the church. The church needs leaders who hold a powerful and challenging vision before the congregation. Leaders dare not allow people to "get by." Good enough was never a standard our Lord Jesus held. In his book, *The Cost of Discipleship*, Dietrich Bonhoeffer wrote, "When Christ calls a man, he bids him come and die."

In Luke 18, a wealthy young man asked Jesus what he must do to inherit eternal life. Jesus reminded him of the commandments. When the man claimed to have followed these since his youth, Jesus said, "There is still one thing lacking. Sell all that you own and distribute the money to the poor, and you will have treasure in heaven; then come, follow me" (v. 22). Jesus made demands on this man. He was held to high standards, and went away sad when challenged by Jesus.

A vision focused on mere survival may not even achieve that. Leaders challenge the congregation by lifting up a vision for the future that is more than the minimum. This might mean calling a full-time pastor or participating in a seminary internship program. It might mean teaching the biblical model of tithing instead of keeping silent about money.

The details of the vision will be unique to your setting but the principle remains consistent. When we are dismissed from Communion, the congregation is sent out into the world with a great challenge, "Go in peace. Serve the Lord." Faithful leaders will offer their congregation concrete ways to live this challenge out with their lives, and the members respond, "Thanks be to God!"

Questions

1. How does your congregation's vision for the future challenge people?

2. What are the most significant challenges facing your congregation today?

3. What opportunities do you provide the congregation to respond to these challenges?

28

Deciding Who Are the Ministers

On Saturday night the high school youth group had a lock-in at the church. They were only there overnight but by Sunday morning the church was in an uproar. Many of the snacks that were purchased and stored in the kitchen for Sunday school that morning were eaten by the youth. The fourth grade Sunday school classroom was left in disarray. The teacher of the adult class had planned to use a video to begin discussion. It took him half an hour of searching for the TV/VCR before he found it in the closet of the youth room, and his video was nowhere to be seen. Who would have thought that twenty high school youth could cause so much chaos in so short a time? To add insult to injury, most of the youth, including their only adult leader, went home to sleep rather than staying for the Sunday morning Communion service.

Now it is Monday evening and the regular monthly congregation council meeting is beginning. This situation will be on the agenda. As a member of the council, how do you react to this challenge?

Choose one or more of the questions below to assist your discussion. Discuss these questions before you continue with "Putting it together."

Questions

1. How do you respond to the situation rather than react?

2. What do you say to congregation council members who are also parents of some of the youth?

3. What are some of the strengths of the congregation that can assist in meeting this challenge?

4. What can you learn from this situation?

Putting it together

Read 1 Peter 2:9-10

> [9]But you are a chosen race, a royal priesthood, a holy nation, God's own people, in order that you may proclaim the mighty acts of him who called you out of darkness into his marvelous light.
>
> [10]Once you were not a people, but now you are God's people; once you had not received mercy, but now you have received mercy.

This sort of challenge can happen in any congregation. Youth groups, even under the best leadership, can cause all sorts of chaos. It is part of what young people do. The challenge before you as a council member is how to use this experience to the benefit of the youth and the church. How can they learn about respect for their church and the fellow members of the body of Christ? How have your church policies or the lack of them contributed to the problem? To what degree is the adult youth leader responsible for the situation?

A careful and thoughtful response will look at the whole picture. It will consider the long-term impact, as well as short-term pain. A faithful response will consider the place for repentance and forgiveness and how you can provide opportunity for both.

The verses from 1 Peter tells us that all the people of God are called to the ministry of proclaiming God's power and love in our lives. Since all are called to serve, how might you include the youth in ministry at your church? Rather than considering youth ministry to only be what you can do for youth, consider it to be those things the youth can do as members of your church. For example:

• Do youth serve on your council?
• Do youth serve as ushers, readers, and assisting ministers in the worship service?
• Do youth teach or assist in teaching Sunday school or vacation Bible school?

- Do youth feed those who are homeless at your local shelter, or help with others as they provide meals?
- What ministry opportunities would move youth across the line from being recipients to being providers of ministry?
- Rather than reacting to this challenge left from a lock-in by laying down the law, how might you respond by inviting youth into gospel ministry?

29

Lead with Patience and Calm

Exodus 16:2-3

> [2]The whole congregation of the Israelites complained against Moses and Aaron in the wilderness. [3]The Israelites said to them, "If only we had died by the hand of the LORD in the land of Egypt, when we sat by the fleshpots and ate our fill of bread; for you have brought us out into this wilderness to kill this whole assembly with hunger."

There were eleven of them sitting around the dining room table. For seventeen years this congregation had been trying to build a new building. The task this evening for these members was to determine if the congregation had the financial capacity to afford the debt that would be necessary to build.

They followed a standard formula to determine their capacity. The results were favorable, and they showed the project could be accomplished.

The floor was opened for comments. John, Luis, and Paula all began to say that this building was not a good idea. In fact they were sure that even though it seemed to be affordable, to continue would mean the end of the congregation. To try and build would mean bankruptcy and the closing of the church.

Other members spoke in favor of the project, pointing out that the present building had significant problems, including no back exit in case of fire. It was very dangerous. A new building would be safer and serve the congregation well. The property was paid for already, and there were substantial savings, so only a bit more than half of the cost would have to be financed.

Two decades and a couple of years later the congregation would celebrate the burning of their mortgage and gather in a beautiful and serving building. Those who were reactive and foresaw only the demise of the congregation were outvoted by those who responded to this opportunity to build.

This is the difference between reacting and responding. Reacting has a long history among the people of God. In the wilderness, Israel begins to complain, to be reactive, accusing Moses and the leaders of bringing them into the middle of nowhere to die. Moses and the leaders do not react, but respond. God sends meat and bread, the famous manna so that the people may eat. Remaining faithful to their calling, Moses and the leaders of Israel are able to respond to the need of the people and at the same time not lose sight of their mission: getting to the promised land.

Reacting is our instinct, before we even think. Reacting comes quickly and naturally. Responding takes thought. Responding takes time and patience. Fear, worry, and anxiety bring reactions. Calm, confidence, and patience bring responses.

In congregations today we still have people reacting. One of the traits of faithful leaders is to respond, not react. Looking to the need, assessing it appropriately, and then seeking the gifts God gives to address such a need are the responsibilities of leadership.

Like those who voted to build a much-needed building and secure a promising future for the congregation above, leaders need to respond, not react.

Questions

1. When have you reacted rather than responded as a leader?

2. When have you taken risks as a leader?

3. How can you lead in a way that includes those who react?

30

Being an Immune System

"Well, it happened again. The pastor made all the visitors stand up and introduce themselves this Sunday. One couple turned so red in the face I bet we never see them again," said Helen. "If that wasn't bad enough she asked Walt Johnson to stand up too. You know Walt only comes with his family a few times a year, but how embarrassing," said Thomas. The education committee's meeting had barely begun and already the conversation was nothing but a list of complaints about the pastor.

After listening to a few more complaints like this, Kathy spoke up: "I am confused. I thought we were here to plan for vacation Bible school and come up with a list of people we might try and recruit to teach Sunday school next fall. If all you want to do is sit and complain about the pastor and this church, I'm going home. I have had a long day already and I have better things to do than listen to complaints."

"But this is important," replied Helen. "How are we going to get teachers and students to VBS this summer if the pastor keeps chasing everyone off?"

Kathy thought for a moment and then responded, "First of all, I support the pastor and all the work she does for our congregation. I do not agree with how she chooses to do everything, but sitting here and talking behind her back will only make things worse. I am here to do my job: plan the educational program of our church. If you have concerns about the pastor and her work, I suggest you deal with her directly. Otherwise I am going home."

The committee grew silent, until Joan began suggesting names for Sunday school teachers. Soon after, the list was complete and they moved on to the business of planning VBS.

Choose one or more of the questions below to assist your discussion. Discuss these questions before you continue with "Putting it together."

Questions

1. If Kathy had not spoken up, how might the meeting have turned out differently?

2. When you are faced with this situation, what prevents you from speaking up? Where do you find the courage to speak up?

3. Why would Kathy have gone home had the committee not regained its focus? What other alternatives did she have?

Putting it together

Read Romans 12:1-2, 9-13

[1]I appeal to you therefore, brothers and sisters, by the mercies of God, to present your bodies as a living sacrifice, holy and acceptable to God, which is your spiritual worship. [2]Do not be conformed to this world, but be transformed by the renewing of your minds, so that you may discern what is the will of God—what is good and acceptable and perfect.

[9]Let love be genuine; hate what is evil, hold fast to what is good; [10]love one another with mutual affection; outdo one another in showing honor. [11]Do not lag in zeal, be ardent in spirit, serve the Lord. [12]Rejoice in hope, be patient in suffering, persevere in prayer. [13]Contribute to the needs of the saints; extend hospitality to strangers.

Complaining is easy to do. It can even be fun to come up with the most outrageous story for the group to chew on. Unfortunately, complaining also serves to distract the group from their real purpose. In this case, Kathy was the one who reminded them why they gathered in the first place. As a leader in the congregation, Kathy reminded the group of their purpose: not complaining about the pastor, but planning VBS and finding Sunday school teachers.

Leaders are called to set appropriate limits on conversation. They are called to define the purpose for gathering and to keep conversation within those limits. There is certainly a place to complain to the pastor. Little good will come from complaining about the pastor, the janitor, the building, or the worship service.

Most of the work in the church is done through volunteers who generously give of their time to serve Christ. After a full day of work, evening meetings that drag on because of irrelevant conversations do not honor people's time. Faithful leaders will hold to an agenda, which thoroughly and promptly addresses the issues at hand.